MW00387548

Money HAS NO COMPLEXION

Money HAS NO COMPLEXION

Finance and Investment Between the Gaps

DR. SCOTT GLENN

gatekeeper press

MONEY HAS
NO COMPLEXION

Published by **Gatekeeper Press**
2167 Stringtown Rd, Suite 109
Columbus, OH 43123-2989
www.GatekeeperPress.com

ISBN (paperback): 9781662924620

DISCLAIMER

I dedicate this book
to the families in the Greenwood District
(Black Wall Street) in Tulsa, Oklahoma, United States of America,
and to all people who have suffered, dealt with,
and overcome the negative effects of
the income and wealth gap.
PRESS ON!

EPIGRAPH

Luke 14:28-30 – Suppose one of you wants to build a tower. Won't you first sit down and estimate the cost to see if you have enough money to complete it? For if you lay the foundation and are not able to finish it, everyone who sees it will ridicule you, saying, "This person began to build and wasn't able to finish."

Proverbs 21:5 – The plans of the diligent lead to profit as surely as haste leads to poverty.

Proverbs 22:7 – The rich rule over the poor, and the borrower is slave to the lender.

Proverbs 21:20 – The wise store up choice food and olive oil, but fools gulp theirs down.

Proverbs 24:27 – Put your outdoor work in order and get your fields ready; after that, build your house.

Ecclesiastes 5:13-14 – I have seen a grievous evil under the sun: wealth hoarded to the harm of its owners, or wealth lost through some misfortune, so that when they have children there is nothing left for them to inherit.

Ecclesiastes 11:2 – Invest in seven ventures, yes, in eight; you do not know what disaster may come upon the land.

(NIV)

FOREWORD

While enrolled in graduate school, I met Dr. Scott Glenn and knew he would be someone who would influence my professional and personal life. Dr. Glenn's demarcation and analysis of genuine leadership is something that I have applied throughout my career. I ascertained from Dr. Glenn that leaders are born and made, and a true leader must grasp how to serve and follow. The greatest opportunity I had in my life was to encounter and know extraordinary people who could challenge and query my way of contemplating and show me a better way. By applying Dr. Glenn's leadership skills, I became an acclaimed leader within my organization and achieved a high level of success. Now, I take every moment as a teachable moment and keep myself humble regardless of my level of accomplishment. For this, I am appreciative and blessed to know and have this influential leader in my life.

Dr. Glenn's *Money Has No Complexion: Finance and Investment Between the Gaps* is an astounding read pervaded with meticulous background knowledge and statistics backed by personal experiences filled with emotional input and perspective by many diverse people. The information and know-how within this book provide one with the "lay terms" and erudition that is not usually presented in the financially frugal and investment books that are available. No matter who reads this book, knowledge will be brought forth and comprehended.

Michael Blackson, Associate Vice President of Surveillance, Nasdaq

FOREWORD

I grew up in a beautiful neighborhood in a big midwestern city enclave populated with old homes abutting a predominantly African American community. My neighborhood and elementary school were diverse. My babysitter's husband was a native American, with a mohawk. My friends came from a spectrum of socioeconomic backgrounds and ethnicities.

In kindergarten, I had my first experience of systemic racism. In school, we were told that because there were too many children in the school, some of the children would be transferred to another elementary school. I was terrified that I'd be forced to leave my school, away from my friends and go to an unknown classroom.

The demarcation of the transfer sent some of the Black children to another school. Relieved that I remained at my school, it wasn't until many years later that I realized that being white afforded me privileges that I did not deserve nor earn.

My father came from abject poverty. His father, my grandfather, was out of work for six or seven years during the Depression. My grandmother sold odds and ends from a cart on the street for many years. My dad began work at age 10 selling newspapers on the street and worked for the remainder of his life. My dad's impoverished upbringing created a tremendous desire for financial success. And due to his relentless work ethic, over time, he built a successful business and created the lifestyle that he aspired to.

My mother began selling real estate when I was in 6th grade and her outgoing personality and tenacity made her a model for me. In a time with fewer women in the workforce, my home modeled the merits of entrepreneurship and hard work.

Money lessons, steeped in my parents' struggles were indelibly embedded in my psyche. From the weekly trips to the bank to deposit part of my $0.50 allowance to the visits to only the lower priced shopping stores, I knew that money was to be conserved and stored. My family lived the "waste not want not" mantra through conservation of all resources, including cut up paper by the telephone for messages in lieu of using a bought pad of paper.

I've worked since age fourteen, babysitting, selling Avon door-to-door, making hippie shirts, and selling to friends in college, tutoring, selling real estate, counseling in a University Career Center, managing money for a private company, freelance financial writing, and finally building a financial-education media company. Working more than one job at a time has been a stalwart of our family's financial success.

Although, as a teen, I felt the conversations surrounding financial success, living conservatively and ways to grow wealth were overly focused on materialism. I even had a short-lived phase where I believed that socialism was the way to go. But those early money lessons have forged my family's future success.

Over the years, I've become struck with how small amounts of money can grow into large sums through the simple process of compounding. Having reached the latter third of life, I've seen firsthand how contributions to my 401(k) 30 years ago, invested in stock, bond, and REIT funds, have multiplied many times over.

It is a documented reality that generational wealth is disproportionately created among White families, for many reasons that Dr. Glenn will discuss. And systemic racist policies that remain to this day are hindering the opportunities for people of color to obtain the best educations and jobs. While the transfer of money knowledge remains disproportionately in the hands of a few, with the rest of the population driven by unhelpful images that suggest you buy now, and buy more, even if you lack the money.

Systemic racism is a greater problem than one book can solve, but understanding the concept and working collectively to call it out and voting to obliterate this societal evil is a step in the right direction.

Money Has No Complexion provides the tools for those without models or mentors to begin the path towards true wealth. First, by understanding the history of the income gap, and then by providing the strategies to build true wealth.

By educating yourself about money from the basics of wants vs. needs, saving vs. spending to investing, you'll have the tools to help change a paycheck-to-paycheck lifestyle. Creating true wealth begins with education. From that financial education, behavioral changes grounded in living beneath your means and saving and investing the difference can point your future towards wealth.

Take the lessons from *Money Has No Complexion*, apply them to your own life, and be patient as the seeds you plant today will bloom into wealth for the future.

Barbara A. Friedberg, MBA, MS, Financial Expert

PREFACE

I write this book from my experience and proficiency in various aspects of business, economics, marketing, and finance as well as a myriad of other subjects related to government, sport, religion, society, finance, and investment. I grew up well-informed about the income and wealth gap in the United States and its effects on people of color, mainly Blacks, due to my rearing and experience. For years, I looked in the mirror at myself and pondered the dearth of people of color in business, education, and other entities. I was concerned about the absence of Blacks in higher education in teaching and top administrative positions and made it the subject of my doctoral dissertation, which was titled *A Qualitative Ethnographic Study of African American Leadership in Higher Education Administration*. The findings of the study were astounding. Despite this knowledge and experience, I was raised not to use these negative circumstances as an excuse and not to point a finger at those who prosper in life, but to persevere no matter the situation, knowing that I would encounter the right people from all walks of life and of diverse ethnicities who would help me to succeed and aid me in my life. I am thankful for all the people I have met on my journey.

On a personal note, in terms of being frugal and comprehending investment, it was not until my twenties that I really understood the need to be frugal and began to realize that although there is a wealth and income gap in the United States, one could make life somewhat better and not worse by making sound decisions in terms of opportunity cost which involves choices. Having said that, one can comprehend how difficult it is even when one is educated about these matters, and yet one is still partially hypocritical in one's frugalness and choices. One important lesson I have learned in life is that no matter what state the world, the country, and society are in, choices or even just one choice or a particular decision will have a profound impact on one's life, even to eternity.

Dr. Scott Glenn

ACKNOWLEDGEMENTS AND SPECIAL THANKS

Much thanks and blessings to the following contributors (appearing in order) who willingly and wholeheartedly participated in providing their knowledge, perceptions, backgrounds, and experience.

Barbara Friedberg, MBA, MS, financial expert.

Trina Edwards, MSN, CEO, Diversity Recruitment Partners.

Scena Webb, DM, educator, Navy veteran, author, entrepreneur, and servant Leader.

Jane Kasumba, broadcaster, lawyer, entrepreneur, and investor (AFRICA).

Ron Hoggard, doctoral candidate, entrepreneur, and nonprofit owner.

Gregory Schwabe, Disabled Veteran and Former Assistant Special Agent of Counter-Intelligence in Korea, Actor, Producer and Executive Producer.

Nitara Lee Osbourne, writer and business owner.

Donald Bradley, retired veteran, United States Marine.

Anthony DiPietro, educator, investor, and registered representative and investment advisor of Voya Financial Advisors.

Rosalind S. Robinson, Doctor of Theology, freelance writer, and editor.

Maria Wood, Luxury Real Estate Broker Associate and REALTOR® with Keller Williams Legacy Realty.

Rod Robinson, Senior Vice President of Insight Sourcing Group, and alumnus of the Wharton School at the University of Pennsylvania.

Cheryl Bowlus, DM, MBAM, entrepreneur

Alison Boord White, Provost and Vice President of Academic Affairs.

Michael Blackson, Associate Vice President of Surveillance at Nasdaq.

TABLE OF CONTENTS

IT'S BEEN A LONG TIME COMING: WEALTH AND INCOME MATTER

In the last 20 years or so, the number of color discrimination filings with the Equal Employment Opportunity Commission has multiplied, showing a rise in community alertness as well as admitting to racial discrimination. Simultaneously, studies devoted to color have improved, and skin tone has become a regular topic in societal studies. Because of this, information about the degree of social stratification by color has increased in contemporary times and appears to be a constant issue, penetrating virtually all facets of the social order (Reece, 2020). This makes one ponder the rationale behind the perspectives and perceptions of many people.

We are all who we are because of our upbringing and factors such as our religious training (or lack of it) and life experiences. When one looks at a 6 and sees it as the number 6, that is what one becomes comfortable with seeing, especially if one has been told and taught about the number 6 before one first sees it. Another person may look at the 6 upside-down and see it as a 9. All things being equal, the person will also agree that the figure is a 9 and be used to the number being just that. Where the dilemma comes in is when both people (who see the number as they do) encounter the opposite. Due to their upbringing, religion, life experiences, and other factors, accepting what they are not used to seeing or are not used to doing may become difficult. While some may understand, others will not. This "69" example is instilled in the thought processes of the world, including in the United States of America, and has had a profound impact on ideologies, mindsets, and the way people are treated.

Graves-Fitzsimmons and Siddiqi (2021) cited the Rev. Susan Hendershot, in explaining that people of faith have the task of creating a more ethical and just world: "We have an extraordinary and historic opportunity to invest in the future we envision, with a safer climate, an equitable and inclusive economy, and modern clean energy infrastructure that improves our daily lives" (para, 8). Graves-Fitzsimmons and Siddiqi (2021) also cited the Rev. Jennifer Butler, CEO of Faith in Public Life Action, on the American Jobs Plan, as saying that leaders of faith, from what they have seen in their communities, believe that for the United States to recover from the COVID-19 pandemic, politicians cannot merely deal with its immediate consequences, but they have to exert themselves to strengthen the economy and society and deal with structural problems and inequalities that existed before the pandemic.

As Congress considers the Biden administration's proposal, they do so comprehending the comprehensive backing that the United States Jobs Plan has amid faith-based communities and concerned citizens of the United States. It would be instrumental in uplifting the country with a more just economy that respects the self-esteem of all workers who contribute to its success.

Graves-Fitzsimmons and Siddiqi (2021) cited a statement by the National Council of Jewish Women who, as an association dedicated to educating women and children, welcomed the president's pledge to rebuild the economy, which they believed would support the needs of women, children, and families, especially the marginalized and people of color.

One cannot fathom the mental perceptions that make people judge or think in a derogatory or biased manner about a person or people due to the color of their skin, yet history is full of examples of how people of color have been discriminated against, creating a plethora of inequalities within the United States from its historical foundation to contemporary times.

The year 2020 proved this inequality and was tremendously stressful for people of color in terms of the pandemic and the social issues going on. One could say the murder of George Floyd along with other societal issues made people of all walks of life more aware of social inequalities and injustices, paving the way for a new administration and way of thinking, including closing the income and wealth gap between people of color and Whites. Vinelli and Weller (2021), Gotanda et al. (2020), and Bell et al. (2017) said that extreme income and wealth inequality and extensive income instability are exacerbated by tenacious and recurrent discrimination. Further indirect prejudices towards people of color and women, for example, mean they receive lower salaries and have less access to assistance and fewer reserves. This exacerbates previous and current tendencies causing additional inequality. These systemic hindrances to people's financial security make it difficult for them to pursue their professions, obtain an education, and start and sustain a business. They cannot completely give their services and aptitudes to the economy. This spectacle of "lost Einsteins," as Bell et al. labelled it, says that discrimination and disparity diminish efficiency and prevent development.

From the days of African American slavery through the Jim Crow era to today, wealth and income disparities have persisted as the gap widens even further and is felt not just in the United States but in communities of color worldwide. The year 2020 was filled with social injustice and traumatic events such as the murder of George Floyd, the Black Lives Matter movement, and attacks on Asians that mirrored the discrimination and turmoil of the 1960s. According to Johnson (2020), the 100 wealthiest people in the United States control more capital than the total Black population, and 96.1% of the 1.2 million families in the upper 1% by income are White. Furthermore, a typical Black household today would need 228 years to achieve the prosperity of a White household (Johnson, 2020). As these disparities continue to increase and attract attention globally, the need for comprehension of financial security and knowledge of investing grows.

> Powell et al (2020) explain, "There is a hunger for fresh approaches and urgent demand for novel policy methods that can break through our political gridlock, address the problems of our time and create new avenues for thriving individuals and communities. Targeted universalism is an approach that supports the needs of the particular while reminding us that we are all part of the same social fabric" (p. 4). More important, the disparity gap can be narrowed only if all stakeholders in the United States are united.

General Systems Theory and Interactive Social System

The general systems theory and interactive social system hold true for organisms and for humans as well because they deal with who we are as people. The general systems theory states that an organism cannot be understood in its lone state while the interactive social system states that organisms, once not alone, understand their being is tied to other organisms and, for the collective group to be successful, they must learn how to operate together. This sounds almost biblical. The general systems theory and interactive social system agree with Genesis and hold true for all organisms, including humans, who are also organisms. We too at times like to be alone, but we're not made to be alone forever. Therefore, like other organisms, we must learn to live together and to cooperate appropriately on the regional and global level. This has proven to be difficult for human beings since the beginning of time. Nonetheless, for the income and wealth gap to lessen, togetherness is needed, and various laws and social constructs from the past must be changed. In the meantime, marginalized people who do not understand appropriate frugality and ways to invest with knowledge and confidence should be aware and cognizant of these aspects.

> Perry and Romer, 2020 posit Tynesia Boyea-Robinson, President and CEO of CapEo explains that, "Fueling Black business growth is broader than just providing capital. It will require leaders in financial institutions, philanthropy, government, corporations, and investors to align and collaborate towards a clear set of goals that address systemic barriers. From supportive policy to representative leadership, it is critical that we work together to build the economy that reflects America's promise" (para 6).

Money Has No Complexion provides sound historical data about the causes of income and wealth gaps and will inspire and help marginalized people of color overcome roadblocks to financial success by providing both quantitative statistical measures and qualitative life experiences and perceptions or perspectives that will provide readers with information and know-how in terms of motivation to "change one's money," achieve financial stability, and make investments with confidence.

This book uses a two-prong approach to providing skills to tackle racial wealth and income disparities. To inspire readers, *Money Has No Complexion* includes numerous stories and anecdotes from people of color who have successfully joined the investor community. The second prong offers compelling, easy-to-understand financial and investment skills. By writing in a conversational yet authoritative style, the authors become mentors and models.

SUMMARY OF CHAPTERS

Chapter 1, **AN ELONGATED HISTORY: THE UNITED STATES INCOME GAP,** provides a detailed historical background with statistical data on how *Money Has No Complexion* will inspire and overcome the roadblocks to financial success, an overview of the income gap between Caucasians and people of color, and an explanation of why people of color have less income than Caucasians.

The second chapter, **FINANCIALLY UNFIT FROM THE START: THE UNITED STATES WEALTH GAP,** thoroughly explains the United States wealth gap and how it can be used to measure the current growth and future existence of people, emphasizing how people of color (Blacks) are generally at a financial disadvantage from the start. The chapter highlights the reasons for the gap such as few opportunities, discriminatory legislation, and racism. The chapter includes statistics and sound data supporting these outcomes, going back to slavery and other discriminatory laws, including mention of the Greenwood District in Tulsa, Oklahoma (Black Wall Street). Chapter 2 furthermore discusses the effects of the wealth gap on mental and physical health and concludes with the untruths about the reasons for the wealth gap while providing real solutions to help close the gap.

Chapter 3, **MONEY CANNOT BUY HAPPINESS: BUT IT CAN HELP IN MAINTAINING LIVING,** demonstrates how to make choices in line with one's values and how one can free up money to save and invest for tomorrow. Readers will learn how to avoid spending to impress and instead focus on dollars and the life circumstances that matter.

Happiness lies in the eye of the beholder, and so do the possession and use of money and its pros and cons. Many may perceive money as the root of all evil. I tend to disagree and believe that the love of money is the root of all evil. How much you have is irrelevant compared to what you do with it! "Money can't buy happiness" might be one of the most ridiculous statements, as anyone without money understands. It is simply common sense that a certain amount of money is necessary to live a comfortable life.

The reader will learn how to figure out the secret recipe to finding the right spending and saving mix to have enough, both now and later. The myth that the latest and greatest stuff leads to happiness is replaced with a plan to decide what is necessary and what is not. Finally, Chapter 3 also explains the mystery of how buying stuff leads to short-lived happiness and conscious spending can lead to both spiritual and financial wealth. The path of identifying what is important guides the reader to live a more meaningful life and become richer.

Chapter 4, **THE FIERCE AND FEARLESS PATH TO FINANCIAL SUCCESS**, introduces the ingredients of financial success such as earning more, budgeting, saving, eliminating debt, and investing. The chapter outlines how these concepts are interrelated and include the trade-offs between spending and investing. Another important concept in investment that is explained is how compound returns can convert a percentage of one's lifetime earnings, invested in financial markets, into a good figure to increase one's net worth. The chapter provides brief introduction to investment assets like stocks, bonds, funds, and other alternatives, along with incorporating stories of how people of color learned to budget, save, invest, and earn more.

Chapter 5 provides knowledge in terms of **WHERE THE MONEY COMES FROM FOR FINANCIAL SECURITY**. It outlines the relationship between income, expenses, saving, and investing and explains why the choices one makes today determine how one will live tomorrow. Chapter 5 then introduces ways to earn more at one's current job and through additional sources of income. Other topics in the chapter include budgeting, automated saving, investing, and lifestyle. The chapter concludes with personal stories of living beneath one's means, budgeting, and spending to design a financially secure future.

Chapter 6, **PUT YOUR PAPER ON THE BIG BOARD: PROFITING FROM THE STOCK MARKET**, may sound scary, but it is not! The chapter takes the mystery out of investing in the stock market. The stock market is not a casino but a path to eliminating financial worries. Learn how simple index fund investing can be practiced by anyone. Discover how to own a piece of the greatest companies in the world and beat the investment returns of most financial professionals. By investing in the stock market, the reader will make more money when global companies grow. Readers learn how to turn $1 into $10 by investing in the stock market.

Imagine if investing could be distilled into a few simple steps. Well, it can. Chapter 6 provides the ultimate knowledge and information that many who misunderstand investments will find relatively elementary. This motivating chapter will explain how readers can go from trading their dollars for a Hershey's chocolate bar to getting paid when anyone, anywhere buys Hershey's candy. TRUST ME! I AM A TRUE PENNSYLANIAN and love the history which extends worldwide. It also shows how investors can mirror how the slower turtle beats the speedy hare in their own money journey. The day trading hares might appear clever, yet the plodding turtles finish richer. Chapter 6 examines the facts about professional investors with index fund investing. The greatest investors in the world, such as John Bogle, founder of Vanguard, and Warren Buffett, recommend the index fund investment route.

Finally, Chapter 6 discusses the keys to unlock the retirement account puzzle. Decipher the IRA, 401(k), 503(b), Roth IRA mysteries and learn how funding these accounts can create hundreds of thousands of dollars for retirement. Learn where, when, and how to open a retirement account.

BE STIRRED AND NOT SHAKEN: EMBRACE BOND INVESTING is the topic of Chapter 7 which briefly explains investing in bonds. It provides a simple explanation of debt investing including types of bonds and bond funds, and why and how to invest in bonds. Real life stories of wealth building with bonds conclude the chapter.

Chapter 8, **BRICK AND MORTAR PAYOFFS: IGNITE YOUR NET WORTH THROUGH REAL ESTATE INVESTING,** is about investment in real estate. The main emphasis is why and how one should invest in real estate, covering the ownership of real property, REITs, crowdfunding, notes, and more. This property chapter concludes with real-life stories of successful motivators, Tony DiPietro, and the amazing Maria Wood.

Investments come in various sizes and for different reaches and wants. Chapter 9 explains the numerous user-friendly alternatives that are available. Titled **INVESTMENT POTPOURRI: THE SWEET SMELL OF SUCCESS FROM ALTERNATIVE INVESTING SOURCES**, it shows that many who think investing is a general clear-cut venture have no idea of the positive opportunities that are involved. Information in this chapter includes less popular ways of investing for tomorrow, the consideration of crowdfunding platforms, cryptocurrency, commodities, investing in businesses, flipping websites, and more. And like the other chapters, it includes alternative investor inspiration from those who have done it.

Chapter 10, **THE POWER OF KNOWLEDGE: COMPREHENDING HOW ENTREPRENEURSHIP AND BUSINESS PLAY A ROLE IN INVESTMENT**, is an explanatory chapter that could have been the first chapter, but I wanted to emphasize the historical facets of the income and wealth gap in the United States. After introducing and explaining the historical aspects as well as the importance of knowledge of frugality and potential investing, the chapter discusses the importance of the power of knowledge in terms of business, frugality, and investment. Chapter 10 emphasizes the importance of comprehending business and entrepreneurship as well as what makes companies successful. This chapter is a book within itself and is the longest chapter.

After the information about business and entrepreneurship, Chapter 11, **DIVERSIFY INVESTMENT OPPORTUNITIES AND LIMIT LOSSES BY CREATING A SHORT- AND LONG-TERM PLAN**, briefly explains how to choose the path that will lead to financial success, including evaluating investment opportunities, understanding losses and gains, diversification, and asset allocation, and rebounding from losses.

Chapter 12, **AFTER WORD**, concludes he book with an afterword and input from the outstanding life experience of the humble and knowledgeable Michael Blackson, Associate Vice President of Surveillance at Nasdaq.

CHAPTER 1

AN ELONGATED HISTORY: THE UNITED STATES INCOME GAP

The income gap in the United States of America will continue to widen unless appropriate action is taken. McIntosh et al. (2020) discussed several factors that created this huge racial gap. It started with slavery which continued for 246 years. The political mishandling of the Freedman's Savings Bank caused 61,144 savers to lose about $3 million in 1874. Bertocchi and Dimico (2010) and Nunn (2007) noted that although slavery was abolished over 150 years ago, research on the influence it had on academic inequality continues. Slavery did not just cause lack of growth in Africa, but correspondingly did so in the United States, and as the decades moved on, African Americans continued to be deprived of a proper education. The mixture of little educational fulfilment and substandard educational value led to huge wage and income gaps. Bertocchi and Dimico pointed out that in the United States, the effects of slavery have been linked more profoundly to regions in the South. This topographical variation permits one to recognize the connection between historical slavery and present disadvantage.

Perea (2014) states that over the decades since the implementation of affirmative action to achieve equality between Blacks and Whites, the Supreme Court has guided the country far away from President Johnson's perception of equality. Instead of viewing affirmative action as a therapy for previous decades of discrimination, contemporary magistrates explain affirmative action as an offensive program that repudiates fairness to Whites.

Although the racial prosperity gap is the result of prejudiced political procedures and laws passed after the Great Depression and Second World War, its cornerstone in slavery and the slave trade dates back to the nation's birth and continued to the latter part of the 19th century. The United States was established on the slave trade, which provided the involuntary and no-cost labor of men, women, and children that permitted White slave owners to build up huge prosperity. If one puts this notion under the microscope in terms of the built wealth opportunity of these owners and the cost to those who provided it, much can be understood (Asante-Muhammad et al., 2017).

The reasons for this barrier or lack of progress have gone unseen because many believe there was major improvement after 1863 and with the Civil Rights Act. They do not understand that each step towards freedom has been met with opposition from those in control who introduced new discriminatory measures to prevent the advancement of Blacks. For example, after slavery was abolished in 1865, prisoner "rental" and sharecropping took place, and after a 10-year battle for civil rights (1863-1873), permissible discrimination (Jim Crow) and disenfranchisement substituted for the former acts (Schermerhorn, 2019a). Graves-Fitzsimmons and Siddiqi (2021) cited Rabbi Victor Urecki of Congregation B'nai Jacob in Charleston, West Virginia:

> Millions are living in poverty, working two or three jobs because wages are so low … There is darkness that is engulfing America. And those in power either do not want to see the pain of those who struggle in the dark or will not leave their homes and extend their arms to the needy (para 7).

Though the G.I. Bill is frequently acclaimed as helping the middle class, such a description is only accurate for White veterans and their relatives since the G.I. Bill's housing benefits assisted only White veterans to buy houses while Black veterans were deprived of the benefit of purchasing houses. The ensuing increase in housing prices has produced massive prosperity for White owners that was denied to African Americans. The events of World War II and the racism that took place during that time provide an accurate foundation for one to look at and evaluate the Supreme Court's affirmative action legal philosophy. Obvious questions remain about what the Supreme Court is saying in relation to what is evident and true in United States history (Perea, 2014).

In addition, obstinate employment market discrimination also pushes Blacks into less gainful jobs than Whites. Therefore, African Americans are less likely to find steady employment, earn less, and have fewer retirement benefits from their employment, which is imperative in terms of acquiring savings for the future. Furthermore, inequalities in the labor market also exist. Chances for African American employees to have employment tenure are way less than for White employees. This is also true in terms of how much money they make which gives the ability to plan for retirement. In 2018, employed African Americans from age 16 and above confronted unemployment almost twice as much as White employees. In addition, part-time employees with lower wages are considerably less likely to have employers that provide retirement plans, with a lot less of participation in these plans. Moreover, racial inequalities in labor market contributions and earnings are not really explained by education or profession either. African American employees at all education levels experience joblessness more than White employees and obtain lower wages at each education level and in each profession (Kijakazi, Smith, et al., 2019).

Political economist Adam Smith said, "The disposition to admire, and almost to worship, the rich and the powerful, and to despise, or, at least, to neglect persons of poor and mean condition is the great and most universal cause of the corruption of our moral sentiments" (inequality.org, 2021, para 15).

Employment and income inequalities are not the consequences of personal failure, but of discrimination and exclusion in appointment, wages, and employment processes that were common and mainly permissible practices through the 1960s, when civil rights lawmaking banned employment discrimination (Kijakazi, Smith, et al. 2019). Having said that, one can still see these aspects such as employment discrimination in all professions and at all job levels. I did a dissertation on this subject entitled *A Qualitative Ethnographic Study of African American leadership in Higher Education Administration.*

> This qualitative ethnographic study involved exploring the educational, background, and professional experiences of senior African American administrators in higher education in the Mid-Atlantic states. The research question that guided the exploration of the experiences and

perceptions of African American administrators in higher education was "What are the professional barriers that slowed the progress of African American employees in higher education obtaining leadership positions as administrators?" (p.12).

The participants, chosen through purposeful selection, were African American (male and female) senior administrators in higher education. Six themes epitomized the main findings of the study: lack of African American representation in higher education administration, lack of African American mentors, underestimating the importance of diversity, insufficient hiring pools, additional job duties, and racial barriers. The recommendations of the study included establishing a sound diversity board, diverse mentoring programs, and diversity awareness. Implementation of the recommendations may change the practices of higher education so that all qualified staff, educators, administrators, and stakeholders can work in a collaborative manner, making the vision, mission, and goals of the institution easier to achieve (Glenn, 2010). Although some strides have been made about this theme, the same lack of representation exists today.

Furthermore, since African Americans are inclined to have lower earnings, the same holds true in acquiring tax benefits even if they own a house and have employment retirement reserves due to the existing tax code which has higher incomes getting greater tax inducements. For families in need, one day's earnings might just take care of that day's basic requirements such as food, clothing, and shelter, but the near future is in jeopardy (Annie E. Casey Foundation, 2016). So that families can comprehend their total potential, savings and assets are considered the money of the future (Bertocchi & Dimico, 2010).

In looking at the influence of slavery on present revenue disparities, it is certainly related to wealth inequality. To put it another way, ex-slave counties suffer greater inequality in contemporary times and display a higher poverty rate and greater racial inequality. The facts show that the effect of slavery on economic inequality and poverty goes through its effect on racial inequality and not the other way around. Bertocchi and Dimico (2010) make use of the land inequality theory, racial discrimination theory, and human capital theory as assessments to comprehend the way in which racial disparities created by slavery affect contemporary income distribution.

MONEY HAS NO COMPLEXION

In terms of land inequality theory, slavery affects contemporary ways of life by way of endowments. Galli and Ronnback, 2021, explain that rising number of findings on historic inequality contend that the origins of inequality in a nation can be drawn back to its initial periods of development, including Colonialism which scholars have branded as a component in inducing inequality. Low counts of housing possession and wages in societies of color mean that these facets will most likely hinder involvement in public gatherings amid people of color. Resident political affairs usually consist of small audiences, and the input of people of color within these societies typically is lessened during elections (Einstein, Glick, and Palmer, 2021). Home ownership is imperative for the economic security and accrual of wealth. Therefore, Families who can buy their own house in the community of their preference at a reasonable price and experience the value of their property increase in time are better off economically in the future. But various programs have systemically discriminated against Blacks who seek to purchase these properties (Rouse, Bernstein, Knudsen and Zhang, 2021).

Racial discrimination theory makes slavery accountable for racial differences in wages and education for African Americans and Whites. The human capital theory claims that the enduring effect of slavery has an adverse influence on human capital accretion for African Americans, by way of an obstinate racial disparity in education. The disparity continues and in many cases is due to the history of slavery and discrimination. In the United States, income and education inequalities are a persistent consequence of slavery, proving that academic disparity is buried deep within the past (Bertocchi & Dimico, 2010).

Inequality.org, 2021 states that in the United States, the revenue gap between the financially wealthy and everybody else has continued to grow for over three decades. Income includes earnings, salaries, interest on savings, payments from shares in various stocks, rent, and revenue from sales. Income numbers, not the same as wealth figures, do not include the worth of property, stock, or other assets. The University of California, Berkeley, data examined by Emmanuel Saez suggest that income inequality denotes revenue that is unequally dispersed amongst a people. In the United States, the upper 10% average over 39 times as much revenue as the lowest 90%, creating extreme revenue disproportions that do not go unnoticed. Although experts have a myriad of ways to explain revenue, they all reach the same conclusion. The upper 1% of the United States employees receive an unequal quantity of revenue in relation to even the country's highest fifth of employees. The Internal Revenue Service statistics show that the greater the income group, the greater the portion of revenue obtained from investment earnings while "non-wealthy" United States citizens receive most of their revenue from salaries and wages. Elongated capital increases due to privileged tax treatment help to create or add to this disparity. Furthermore, Bureau of Labor Statistics (2021) data show how racial discrimination in many areas such as academia, employment, and renumeration procedures aids in the continuous widening of earnings gaps.

Schermerhorn (2019 a) states that Blacks who took part in the Second World War not only battled the "enemy" abroad but also returned to discrimination in the United States, including "false" or no benefits from the G.I. Bill. Schermerhorn emphasized the importance of social security benefits for agricultural workers, saying how Blacks who were already hard hit financially could not obtain these benefits. The G.I. Bill caused half of the country's college and university admission to be filled by veterans who would benefit from the bill, passing on the results to their siblings and their children who followed in their educational footsteps, aiding the path to attractive employment in management and administrative settings rather than tougher physical and unskilled labor. This educational benefit that Blacks were excluded from continues to have an adverse impact on succeeding generations of Blacks. White prerogative and antipathy led to many Blacks, who lacked benefits and opportunities, being jailed. Continued discrimination impeded Black opportunity as the justice system and its politics time after time made imprisonment a lifelong economic verdict for Black people who were convicted (Pew Charitable Trusts, 2010). Sankar-Bergmann and Shorter (2016) stressed that in contemporary United States society, 70-100 million United States citizens have a criminal record. Nellis (2016) said that societies with people of color include an unequal number of the imprisoned populace and these societies are inclined to be sucked into the prevalent criminal justice system, a system in which more than half of inmates from 12 states are African Americans and Latinos. Hagler (2015) explained that the criminal justice system's influence on racial disparities in terms of wealth cannot be overlooked, knowing that such aspects as financial liability created by a system of charges and payments can often create a financial burden for people who have gotten caught up in the system due to financial circumstances even beyond paying debts to the community and being exonerated from their crime.

Perea (2014) claimed that government policy after World War II furthered discrimination against Blacks in education and housing. The G.I. Bill proves that the government overtly encouraged housing discrimination against Blacks. The G.I. Bill purposely left the administration of national schooling and housing assistance to colleges and universities, privatized banks, realtors, and White home proprietors' associations, each of whom discriminated willingly and persistently against Blacks. This was done to appease the requests of political representatives in the South to keep their structure of racial segregation, as happened during the New Deal under President Roosevelt. Federal acceptance of discrimination against Blacks is alive, verifiable, and irrefutable. There is no stronger violation of equality than the racism of the national government in backing privilege for Whites and discrimination against Blacks.

CHAPTER 2

FINANCIALLY UNFIT FROM THE START: THE UNITED STATES WEALTH GAP

Wealth is the most comprehensive measuring rod of a person or family's growth and prospects for the future. Even with extended education, being African American means having less wealth than Whites which translates into fewer chances to advance in life and being assigned to lower strata of society with less likelihood of growing wealth and passing accrued wealth down to the next generation of family members. Many factors worsen and contribute to this malicious cycle, such as Black families having fewer opportunities and access to tax privileged reserves because of a history of job discrimination and other discriminatory practices (Inequality.org, 2021).

Education plays a vital role in economic progress. During a lifespan, United States citizens with postsecondary degrees make 84% more than people with just a secondary diploma (Carnevale et al., n.d.). The racial wealth gap persists also for Blacks who are well educated and come from homes with two adults. Black people with graduate or professional degrees have $200,000 less than correspondingly educated Whites (Traub et al., 2017).

Income largely comprises money individuals make as a result of employment while wealth is demarcated as the difference between savings (like savings and retirement accounts) and home ownership and debt. Economic experts have determined that wealth is even more unequally dispersed than income in the United States

(Thompson & Weller, 2016). The United States displays broader inequalities of prosperity between the wealthy and underprivileged than any other industrialized country. Research on inequality in the United States mainly emphasizes income while there is less information about wealth inequality mainly due to the dearth of reliable statistics. The Opportunity and Inclusive Growth Institute explained the disparity of income and wealth with innovative statistics created from past studies and showed that wealth in terms of stocks and housing has remained a vital aspect of inequality in the United States for over seven decades (Clement, 2018).

Amadeo (2020) stated that the Corporation for Enterprise Development explained that although the federal government policies dynamically endorse the building up of wealth, it has a profound impact on people of color. Annually, government proposes about $347.8 billion in tax slashes intended to build wealth. Within these slashes, about 39.2% encourage homeownership whereas 41% funds savings and investment. Amadeo (2021) said that research conducted in 2015 showed that reducing the homeownership gap would tighten the ethnic prosperity gap by 31%.

The Annie E. Casey Foundation (2016) explained that the government has offered enticements to households to help gain assets through the nation's past. However, the plans delivered such as retirement assets from tax aid to housing interest subtracted are actions that excessively profit people with properties and provide minute help for people with little earnings and funds.

As one can see, these slashes aid affluent people much more than the underprivileged. The richest 5% of United States citizens are in the best economic situation to benefit from these tax slashes, acquiring 53% of the $347.8 billion. The people earning $50,000 or less, representing the bottommost 60%, get just 4% of these tax slashes while people making $19,000 or less, the lowest 20%, get a measly 0.04% (Woo et al., 2010).

The court of law's course has undone affirmative action from its societal and historic framework as well as its main reasoning (Perea, 2014). This degenerating cycle causes certain hindrances for people of color, who are likely to possess investments and are less likely to have savings or hereditary capital. Household assets are correlated with pointers of a youngster's healthy state which includes various facets like educational routine and self-confidence as well as helping young people avoid adverse predicaments like relationship problems and adolescent pregnancy (Annie E. Casey Foundation, 2016).

The Federal Reserve's distributional financial accounts show that the affluent do not just consume more capital than everybody else. Most of their prosperity is derived from various and more profitable assets (https://www.federalreserve.gov/releases/z1/dataviz/dfa/distribute/chart/). The United States top 1%, for example, embraces more than half the nationwide wealth invested in stocks and mutual funds. Most of the wealth of United States people in the lowest 90% is derived from their houses (Inequality.org, 2021). Schermerhorn (2019 b) noted that in the two years before the end of the Civil War, African Americans possessed 0.5% of the countrywide financial prosperity.

Asante-Muhammad et al. (2017) and Coates (2014) stated that up to 1860, the lower Mississippi Valley produced more millionaires per capita than any other place in United States. Ethnically selective land-dwelling relocation required by the Homestead Act, meant that about 270 million acres, around 10% of all land-dwelling in the United States, was provided to more than 1.6 million homesteaders. In contemporary times, studies find 46 million adults, around 20% of the country's population, can possibly look back at their people's past of building prosperity to this single civic policy.

In the contemporary United States, the dearth of wealth has only risen 0.5% for roughly the equivalent percentage of the general populace, and an typical Black household has a slim one tenth of the financial prosperity of the representative White household. Inequality.org (2021) states that wealth can be explained as net worth and the quantity of all assets subtracted form liabilities. In the United States, wealth inequality is more noticeable than income inequality. Hanks et al. (2018) suggested that wealth can be described as the measure of economic value of a person or family which is key to a myriad of opportunities for United States family members. Financial wealth is significant in terms of progression in employment, home living or ownership, as well as emergency measures in various circumstances.

Schermerhorn (2019 a) says, in the past decades, new regulations were shaped by the United States government in favor of Whites, generating economic privileges for the White population. Housing and property specialists and developers worked together to formulate discriminatory loaning procedures that put Blacks in tough situations and living areas where social problems compounded other dilemmas like poor educational facilities as well as a lack of amenities that make ascending mobility in life challenging or nonexistent. In 1954, the Brown v. Board of Education Supreme Court ruling decided that school segregation was unconstitutional, but educational institutions tracked local neighborhood borders, and neighborhoods were segregated (Amadeo, 2020).

Various acts such as the Homestead Act also limited Blacks tremendously. Shapiro (2004) said that even though the Homestead Act allowed all adults including Blacks to acquire property, the act still excessively profited White families. Williams (2003) says that it is imperative to admit that the Homestead Act was possible because land was taken by the United States government from Native peoples, adding to the list of wrongs in U.S. history including the killings, deceptions, and involuntary evictions that have prevented Native peoples from flourishing in contemporary times.

The social security program was ratified in 1935 as part the New Deal made by President Roosevelt. The law has been explained as color blind since race is not part of the reason that the law was made. The only problem is that the original decree was just for employees who were working on a regular basis in the field of business and manufacturing and excluded domestic employees and farmers who were not protected by the regulation. Asante-Muhammad et al. (2017) cited the U.S. Census Bureau (2015), saying that even though social security safety programs are created to help people through poverty, many of these programs in which mainly Blacks and people of color rather than Whites are involved are controlled and do little in terms of asset savings to enable people to move ahead in life.

About 65% of African American employees were employed in the two jobs omitted in 1930 (DeWitt, 2010). Many experts contend that the choice to eliminate these employees was ethnically driven and that members of Congress from Southern states sought this action for African American sharecroppers to stay under the control of White homestead proprietors, having no other means of being employed except with insufficient earnings (Quadagno, 1988; Stoesz,

2016). African Americans were omitted from social security due to the coalitions amongst White politicians that intersected regions and party-political lines, with President Roosevelt's Committee on Economic Security, which was responsible for making the social security system (Poole 2006). Regardless whether the choice to eliminate domestic employees and farmers from the social security coverage was ethnically prejudiced or not, the plan made a structural wall that ended in an unequal portion of African American laborers being omitted from coverage, unlike White employees. Even though African Americans composed up to 11.3% of the workforce in 1930, they made up 23% of the employees that were not protected when social security was endorsed (DeWitt, 2010). Social security improvements should emphasize working positively to help people in need and not hurting them in terms of caregiver credit, spouse and child benefits, retirement age, taxable wage, and cost of living adjustment. The majority of African American employees were not protected by the social security program in the beginning, but changes to social security over time have made it a common and essential part of economic security for countless African Americans. Nevertheless, ethnic and gender discrimination that continues in the labor market adds to racial disparities in social security assistance levels that keep an unequal portion of African Americans in poverty (Kijakazi, Smith, et al., 2019).

The Annie E. Casey Foundation (2016) states that assets like savings, an education fund, and house ownership offer the economic stability and enable families to help their children realize their dreams. This available money is also a "security blanket" in times of unexpected need such as sickness or an automobile problem that can lead to debt. In reference to housing and ownership, equity is composed of around two-thirds of average home financial prosperity and preventing African Americans from acquiring this equity in a period when housing worth was prosperous, further hurt Blacks and ensured that the wealth gap continued (Schermerhorn, 2019 a).

Constant housing and employment market discrimination and segregation fueled the destructive process of wealth inequality. In the past, discrimination in the housing loan market was a result of Blacks being less likely to be able to become proprietors of homes than Whites, which resulted in them having less admittance to the reserves and tax assistance that accompany possessing a property or a house (Inequality.org, 2021).

Perry and Romer (2020), explain, "the analysis of the American Business Survey in saying that 90% of new businesses among all races do not receive any outside investors. Most people use the equity in their homes to start their firms. Prior Brookings research has shown devaluation of property in Black neighborhoods, which throttles this method of business development. Homes in Black neighborhoods across the country are devalued by an estimated sum of $156 billion—the equivalent of more than 4 million firms, based on the average amount Black people use to start their businesses. Declining home ownership rates also hamstring Black business growth" (para 9).

The first World War and the Great Migration to the North of the United States, Blacks were confronted with additional hurdles in terms of opportunities such as housing, including extreme fees and other systematic predispositions and bias. Black arithmetician and sociologist Kelly Miller said in 1930, "The Negro is up against the white man's standard, without the white man's opportunity" (Schermerhorn, 2019 a, para.7). During the Great Migration, Blacks did their best to abide by the rules to acquire the American Dream, but discrimination from their Southern past shadowed them and resurfaced in national housing assistance programs and other public policies which were guided by Democrats from the South who had a strong hold and influence on the New Deal regulations (Schermerhorn, 2019 a). Countless White Americans still profit from the federal government's racism of past decades, but approximately two thirds of Whites hold differing opinions and do not think they have profited from historical and contemporary discrimination against African Americans, despite the clear record of history that Whites in general profited immensely from this racial discrimination (Perea, 2014).

Hanks et al. (2018) suggested this gap exists not only for African Americans, but it is widened in terms of Hispanics, Asians, and Pacific Islanders as well. Hispanic people wealth wise are a touch ahead of Black families. In 2016, the average wealth for Black and Hispanic people was $17,600 and $20,700, respectively, in relation to White peoples' average wealth of $171,000. The Black and White wealth gap is due to deliberate orderly procedure and political decisions, and the only way to fix it is to produce calculated sound changes (Hanks et al., 2018). Perea (2014, p. 583) quoted Lyndon B. Johnson:

You do not take a person who, for years, has been hobbled by chains and liberate him, bring him up to the starting line of a race and then say, "You are free to compete with all the others," and still justly believe that you have been completely fair. .... This is the next and the more profound stage of the battle for civil rights. We seek not just freedom but opportunity. We seek not just legal equity but human ability, not just equality as a right and a theory but equality as a fact and equality as a result. .... To this end equal opportunity is essential but not enough, not enough.

The economic security of African Americans falls way short of the United States populace as a whole, especially the White population. The explanations are multifaceted, but one aspect that is imperative and worth noting is the augmented economic literacy of African Americans. Modest pecuniary pointers exemplify this disparity with 66% of African Americans claiming that they are barely living "above water" (financially) compared to analogous statistics among Whites at 78%. Average family income among African Americans was $35,400 in 2016 while average family income of Whites was $61,200. African American family net worth was $17,600 in 2016 and 19% had zero or negative net worth; the corresponding statistics for White families were $171,000 and 9%, respectively. To look specifically at these numbers, the use of the P-Fin Index can provide a clearer picture of this growing gap so that individuals within the African American society can comprehend finance and investing and how to make use of their economic condition. The P-Fin Index scales personal finance information and comprehension in eight practical parts consisting of earning, consumption, saving, borrowing, insurance, and investing types of risks, ambiguity, and outcomes (Yakoboski, 2021).

Racial variances in wealth are particularly obvious. Asante-Muhammad et al. (2017) noted that Policy Link printed an examination that gave for the first time an estimate of which racial groups profit most from tax disbursements. Within this study, scholars discovered that White families epitomized the mainstream of revenue recipients in all revenue quintiles, plus involving the highest three quintiles. If there is no change to help support people of color in terms of this matter, especially African Americans and Latinos, the gap will continue, and matching of wealth to Whites will not occur for centuries as it would take 228 years for the typical Black household to catch up to what Whites possess in contemporary times. In reference to Latino households, matching the wealth of Whites would take about 84 years. As for Native American statistics, the dilemma for this society is not about how they are seen, but if they are noticed at all. Although economic statistics about Asian families are frequently askew, Native American economic statistics are mostly obsolete and hard to gather as well as inadequate. In general, their circumstances in relation to African Americans and Latinos are analogous and perhaps even worse. African Americans and Latinos are inclined to have less prosperity than Whites. The current prosperity gap has continued as economic mobility as well as the capability to save has disappeared for countless individuals, particularly African Americans and Latinos. The statistical evidence that the typical Asian American family has a greater hierarchy in academic fulfilment and lesser wealth than the typical White family implies that the disparities are not solely restricted to demographics like age and region, but the variances mirror prevalent and extended inequality amid other economic pointers such as employment, earnings, and benefits and assistance among Asian American subclasses (Thompson & Weller, 2016).

Repudiating Admittance to the Asset of Citizenship, the Chinese Exclusion Act was ratified in 1882, placing a decade ban on Chinese employees settling in the United States becoming natural citizens to conciliate financial and social anxieties raised by White Americans during this period. The Chinese immigrant experience is not exceptional for people of color, many of whom have been denied citizenship. Racial discrimination in immigration policy was normal from 1790 to 1965, yet immigration laws still use race to justify discrimination, even though granting citizenship on the basis of race is now illegal (Asante-Muhammad et al., 2017).

Some studies are available on the distribution of wealth among United States Asian families, and this continues to be a topic targeted for research. Few studies in terms of wealth inequality exist on the distribution of wealth among Whites and Asian Americans, but research is imperative since Asians are the fastest growing ethnic group in the United States. While numerous Asian Americans have wealth comparable to that of Whites, a great number of Asian Americans have little or no wealth (Thompson & Weller, 2016).

MONEY HAS NO COMPLEXION

The struggles of Asian American societies with economic inequality are frequently unnoticed due to usual stereotypes and the overview of economic statistics, which places 21 million ethnically diverse individuals from 48 countries, each with different perspectives of immigration and wealth, into a sole group. This merging further maintains the "model minority" allegory of Asian families as being clearly better off than other societies of color.

Native Americans are composed of a diverse populace which exists in the city as well as in the country and rural areas. They are composed of several ethnic groups including affiliates of tribes and those who are not. For many native American societies, living with constant ethnic economic disparity is a way of life.

The United States many times has hindered Native American progress. Over the decades of deliberate legislative procedures that removed domains and properties, Native Americans have lost the prosperity and possessions that were legally theirs. Therefore, Native Americans, persons from a myriad of indigenous groups of North, Central, and South America, remain marginalized within a racial prosperity gap, just as Latinos and African Americans are. The utmost economic inequality for Native Americans is found within the reservations themselves. The average salary on a reservation is $29,097, compared to the nationwide average pay for Native Americans which is $40,315. (Muhammad et al. 2019).

The Greenwood District ("Black Wall Street")

In terms of thriving in business, the brutal annihilation of a populace of 10,000 Black people in the Greenwood District of Tulsa, Oklahoma, 100 years ago is included in this book as one of the many tragedies of people of color in terms of acquiring wealth and income.

Perry et al. (2021) explain that racial conflict in Tulsa, Oklahoma, may have been inevitable, mainly because of the factions in the community during the Jim Crow era. Greenwood was feasibly the plushest Black society in the United States, and neighboring White communities viewed its economic success as a threat. The horrible events of 1921 arose with scooped up rape accusations of a Black inhabitant, in the local White newspaper. This rapidly proceeded to warnings of lynching and conflicts between Black people trying to safeguard themselves and Whites trying to take matters into their own hands.

Perry et al. (2021) continue to say that before the incident in Tulsa, Oklahoma, the Greenwood District was a prosperous Black middle-class area, including a vigorous home-grown Black economy with cash flowing among Black people, Black banks, and Black businesses. Like Memphis' Beale Street, Greenwood was a thriving Black district at a time when the tyrannical Jim Crow system forced Black communities to produce and uphold their personal capital, mainly cut off from the larger macro economy. In the outcome of the annihilation, state and federal politicians and the private sector were astute in depicting the incident as a "race riot," which assisted them to elude responsibility to help restore the district. The Tulsa Historical Society and Museum calls the destruction a "riot" which was the excuse that insurance companies used to evade compensating proprietors who lost land and property.

The Greenwood Cultural Center notes that the region did not obtain any compensation or reconstruction cash from the local, state, or federal government. Actually, the nearby White communities were aggressive towards the idea of reconstructing Greenwood, as evinced by a Tulsa newspaper report that stated "the old 'Niggertown' must never be allowed in Tulsa again" (Sidner, 2016, para. 1). Nonetheless, and beating the probabilities, Greenwood's Black inhabitants were proficient to gather their residual possessions to re-erect the region in a few years, regardless of the dearth of external funding regulated by Jim Crow laws and banks. The district prospered through the 1960s to the 1980s until decisions by White city organizers demolished it again in what the Human Rights Watch called "urban renewal." This included a call for reparations due to a combination of procedures that involved rezoning and freeway structure which led to plummeting land values, while prejudiced redlining procedures disallowed the instillation of firsthand capital into the society.

The *American Journal of Economics and Sociology* in 2018 evaluated the absolute monetary effect of the 1921 massacre stating, "If 1,200 median priced houses in Tulsa were destroyed today, the loss would be around $150 million ...The additional loss of other assets, including cash, personal belongings, and commercial property, might bring the total to over $200 million" (as cited in Perry et al., 2021, para 23).

My Experience: Black Wall Street

During the July 4th weekend of 2021, my wife and I traveled across the country, and one of our stops was the Greenwood District in Tulsa, Oklahoma. As we crossed the Missouri border to Oklahoma on a beautiful warm sunshiny day, we could not help noticing the beautiful scenery as we drove through the turnpike which was clean and immaculate. It appeared as the brown dirt began to turn a sultry red and the green brush bristled in the sunlight, giving us a delightful feeling of comfort and joy as we continued to drive through Oklahoma. I can still remember the nice people as we stopped to rest as well as numerous signs announcing the Cherokee Nation, of which I am a descendent, but I had no idea how prominent they were in that part of Oklahoma. Oklahoma City, Broken Arrow, and the various major colleges and universities were all in our thoughts as we reminisced. As we drove past the tornado stricken town of La Jolla, we thought about the victims and pondered what it must have been like to be affected by this category 5 tornado. The trip was full of emotions, both joyful and upsetting, as we experienced these sights. Late in the afternoon, we reached Tulsa. Knowing we had to get up early in the morning to continue our journey, we decided to visit "Black Wall Street!" Traveling about 10 minutes down the highway from our hotel, we came upon a shocking sight. A huge mural of Blacks retreating in terror from burning buildings caught our eye first and then the actual memorial. As we took pictures of the area, I could feel the hurt and pain of what happened not just that day in Greenwood, but throughout history in terms of the turmoil and discrimination that Blacks and many minorities have encountered over the years. Among these feelings, we thought of the families who owned business in that area who had amazing stories of recovery and motivation which helped somewhat to heal the emotions we were experiencing. Numerous White people were also paying respect and honor to this historical site as they hugged each other and Blacks, which was an amazing sight to see. This action provided a reminder that from the days of slavery and before, some Whites played a crucial role in helping minorities and still do today. Many times, people are put into boxes. Throughout our trip across the country and in our interactions with a multitude of people, we found in general that people are good, and although much improvement is needed, times are better than in previous decades.

McIntosh et. Al., (2020) stated that bigoted political procedures in the 20th century like the Jim Crow laws or Black Codes severely restricted the chance of growth in the South for Blacks. Furthermore, the G.I. Bill left out a large number of African Americans who could not profit from its benefits. President Roosevelt's New Deal (Fair Labor Acts) discriminated against Blacks in terms of domestic farming and service jobs. Finally, keeping Blacks from getting financial help due to their poor status and living areas also hindered their ability to advance in life. All these effects explain the general reasons for the wealth gap and how opportunity was stripped from these societies which stopped them from prospering. In modern times, this history is of substance because the inequality still exists and is a legacy handed down through generations by way of unequal financial inheritances. United States citizens in 2020 are expected to receive inheritance around 765 billion which comprises wealth transferences to married persons and transfers that fund children. Bequests make up about 4% of the yearly family revenue, a lot that is not taxed by the government.

Muhammad et al. (2019) stated that the 2018 United States Census posted by Poverty USA showed that Native Americans top the list of minorities with the largest poverty rate (25.4%) ahead of African Americans (20.8%) and Hispanics (17.6%), while Whites had an 8.1% countrywide poverty rate. In general, generating more financial security and chances for all United States citizens, including Asians, is simply an action of politically awareness (Thompson & Weller, 2016). At the end of the business quarter in 2020, the average White employee profited 27% more than the average Black employee and 36% more than the average Latinx employee. Unequal distribution of income does not just have a bearing on the wealth of a country, but disparity correspondingly helps decipher the well-being of a nation in terms of health (Inequality.org, 2021).

Inequality: Mental and Physical Health Effects

Former member of Congress Shirley Chisholm once said, "We have never seen health as a right. It has been conceived as a privilege, available only to those who can afford it. This is the real reason the American health care system is in such a scandalous state" (Inequality.org, 2021, Quotes, para 7). There is a strong correlation between inequality of income and wealth in terms of health. Many experts globally explain that greater financial inequality results in poor physical well-being, affects life expectation, contributes to child mortality, and causes obesity. Economists and the World Health Organization agree that the causes of inequality creating poor living conditions equate to a shorter life span. An American Psychological Association report provided research that says United States families with a yearly revenue under $50,000 have greater anxiety than other people as the divide between the wealthy and underprivileged expands.

The *Journal of the American College of Cardiology* (2019) says that greater levels of income inequality are tied to greater risks and rates of circulatory-associated deaths and hospital care. Moreover, University of Oxford Business School research emphasizes that severe inequality tends to affect how individuals see themselves. In countries in which the top 1% have the higher portion of revenue, the people display less individual well-being. There is also a connection between inequality and mental health, and nations with greater gaps between the wealthy and underprivileged have higher rates of schizophrenia.

Conceivably, the greatest effect of racial inequalities in social security is in relation to health issues in people's surroundings that affect their well-being. Studies show that health inequalities continue between African American and White people (Assari, 2018). Research shows that structural racism and discrimination in employment, earnings, and professions as well as in academia, housing and financial asset accumulation hurt health and are the main causes of health disparities (Assari, 2018; Jones, 2000; Smedley, 2007; Williams, 2003). Williams contends that "structural racism is the most important way through which racism affects health" (p. 107). Structural racism means African Americans get rarer health advances than White people from the shielding results of surges in resources like education and employment (Assari, 2018). Although adjustments have been made for socioeconomic standing, racial variances in well-being continue (Williams, 2003).

The American Psychological Association report furthermore explained that blue-collar or low-wage employment is usually more demanding on the individual than white-collar employment. This adds to a multitude of extra well-being complications such as back problems, high blood pressure, and high blood sugar levels. In addition to these physical ailments, various social aspects also affect these people in all sorts of forms of discrimination. The Center for Economic and Policy Research also supports this inequality effect with sound facts, stating that those at the bottom of the United States employment ranking on the country's economic hierarchy are more likely to be employed with over-challenging employment conditions, creating psychological and physical strain. In addition, these people have greater health bills and stop working earlier, forcing them not to partake in the full benefits of social security which the Brookings Institute says is common among these people who are senior citizens (Inequality.org, 2021).

Countless individuals consume minimal to no wealth whereas many others have accumulated extensive quantities. Wealth inequality is characteristically considerably greater than income inequality. Statistics show that those who are currently "below water" economically also are inclined to indulge in ambiguous futures. The gap between the wealthy and deprived continues, and those who are currently prosperous most likely will have a protected financial future where those who are behind will not (Thompson & Weller, 2016).

Financial health is contingent in many instances on how soundly people navigate the numerous financial choices that confront them in the typical path of life. Financial literacy is information and comprehension that permits sound financial decision making and actual managing of individual finances. Therefore, financial literacy is imperative to an individual's economic well-being (Yakoboski, 2021). The statistics show that African American knowledge in terms of financial literacy continues to have a profound impact on their decision making and affects their overall well-being, including their health. The Index Indicator mentioned is a sound gauge and tool to measure these aspects, but the use of actual experience and stories coupled with the statistics is missing.

Untruths and Falsehoods: Reasons for The Gaps

Darity et al. (2018) stated that many claim that the wealth gap can be shrunk by improving organization in families and changing the way Black people conduct their lives. It is claimed that they need to be more accountable, which includes gaining financial knowledge, education, and employment skills. Blacks need to own homes, Black purchasing and Black investment must increase, and Blacks need to improve their personal savings, engage in entrepreneurship and grow their businesses, and copy the achievements of other Blacks. Some even claim that the growing number of Black celebrities proves the racial wealth gap is closing. These things do help to close the gap but are not major reasons for the gap and are inadequate to bridge it.

Darity et al. continues by stating that education and employment skills are imperative to all families, but at every educational level, Black people's average wealth is way less than that of Whites. White people with a bachelor's degree or advanced doctoral degree are much wealthier than Blacks with the same degree. In terms of owning houses, Blacks who do not own a house have a meager $120 in terms of net value which is not enough to provide the essentials such as food to the household. The statistics show that White families who do not own a house have 31 times more prosperity than Black families in terms of entrepreneurship and business.

Therefore, with the obstacles to building Black prosperity and the sustained exclusion of Blacks from professional credit markets, admittance to the required resources to accumulate wealth is not available. The only way of helping Black's progress, steamrolling the playing field of racial wealth disparities while simultaneously growing Black start-up and progressive money is changing the economic structures, racism, and White authority of American society. Darity et al. (2018) and Traub et al. (2017) claim that according to the Institute on Assets and Social Policy, Black people in general live more frugally in terms of savings than Whites. Statistics from 2013 showed that, at similar stages of salary, Whites spend 1.3 times more compared to Blacks. However, the mindset that Blacks waste money was created by President Ronald Reagan in the 1980s when he used the term "welfare queen" and in contemporary times by pictures on the internet of Blacks in the United States paying for athlete Michael Jordan's Nike apparel instead of home necessities. However, the evidence says the antithesis—that Blacks, historically and today, are more careful with money than Whites.

Entrepreneurship in a big measure can have a profoundly negative impact on existing businesses, and it also can heighten the wealth divide between the rich and the poor. Data gathered show that people of marginalized societies who can get into the entrepreneurship arena tend to fail because of such aspects as lack of money and inadequate access to the market (Darity et al., 2018).

Derrick Johnson, President and CEO of the NAACP explains the importance of Black entrepreneurship, "Investments that don't strategically consider place and sector are not real investments; it's charity. Black communities and entrepreneurs across the U.S. need investments to reach specific industries in particular regions to maximize growth" (Perry and Romer, 2020, para, 23).

Financial and investment knowledge is imperative, and one should by no means neglect this due to the large gap that exists between Whites and minorities. Finance and investment may not close the gap, but having sound knowledge and know-how to save, make sound financial decisions, and the ability to invest at one's own level can help tremendously. This is the reason for writing this book: To provide the proper know-how in finance and investment so that people can be positively confident within their economic circumstances, no matter what financial hand is dealt to a person or family. Darity et al. further clarified that the main fact is Whites normally have more resources to invest at the outset and that they do not just invest more in housing but much more in economic assets as well.

Perry and Romer, 2020, say that the United States Census Bureau contemporary statistics state that Black people encompass roughly 14.2% of the U.S. population, but Black businesses encompass only 2.2% of the country's 5.7 million employer businesses (more than one employee). We can't foresee what would occur if racism was detached from numerous markets, but if Black businesses dispatched alike statistics to non-Black businesses, the nation would comprehend noteworthy economic progression.

Essentially, Whites acquire more assets due to having more access to resources as one can see that prosperity produces more prosperity. In addition, greater wealth permits more access credit along with economic choice and security to take investment risks and protection from the risk of financial damage. Therefore, having outstanding financial status and knowledge is valued if one has the finances to do so. To sum it all up, having economic knowledge in investment without actual money is worthless since there is no fairytale method to convert no prosperity into excessive prosperity just by acquiring more financial knowledge (Darity et al., 2018).

Just as having knowledge about finances and investment without money or a sound economic condition cannot bring enchanted wealth, the same holds true about trying to copy other minorities who have been successful. The chances of success are slim to none. The belief that disparities in wealth between groups are the result of cultural or behavioral deficiencies is misleading. Rather, low-wealth racial and ethnic groups have experienced a long history of having their wealth taken from them and barriers to accumulating wealth. Regrettably, many top minority celebrities have concealed Black poverty relative to helping to reduce the racial prosperity gap.

Home Environment

The ever-growing number of one-parent homes, including the mother who is not married, is often considered a main reason for the growth of inequality. This claim tends to obscure the truth and is mainly motivated by the belief that if Blacks modify their way of life, a surge in prosperity will occur. This notion is dangerous and imbedded in racist stereotypes. In terms of a couple being married, statistics show that marriage does not help close the gap or balance prosperity for White and Black women who have postsecondary diplomas. Darity et al. (2018) and Traub et al. (2017) agree that married White women without a four-year degree have in excess of two and a half times the prosperity of married Black women with a four-year degree. Darity et al. continue that ethnic prosperity inequalities broaden amongst married women with a four-year degree. White women who are married and live in a house have five times or more the total prosperity of Black women. In addition, White families with a single White parent have a total worth two times greater than that of Black married couples. Johnson (2020) says according to Brian Thompson, a contributor to Forbes.com, the term "systemic racism" irritates many people. It frequently initiates sensitive debates about how individuals feel about racism and the impact it has on people. However, statistics over extended periods provide strong evidence that systemic racism happens and continues to be real (Johnson, 2020). The United States economic system is backed by detrimental accounts involving inadequate admittance to assets which causes unequal chances to preserve or grow prosperity to be passed on to family members in the future. We as a nation must carry on past these misconceptions and face the causes of these gaps.

Closing the Disparity Gap

Harmful social policies have shaped and preserved the racial wealth gap, and only a radical change in direction can reduce it. Academic achievement, the right profession, and full-time employment are essential, but even if these were made equal among the races, this would not be adequate for creating prosperity (Jones, 2017). To correct these inequalities, we as a nation must remember what Nelson Mandela once said, "We must work together to ensure the equitable distribution of wealth, opportunity, and power in our society" (Quotes, para 4).

Politicians could also increase wealth by eliminating some of the debt of individuals by removing the necessity for them to borrow. This can be done by trimming the cost of education and lowering the interest on loans (Thompson & Weller, 2016). Tax reforms such as inheritance, capital gains, and wealth taxes could reduce the gap and improve equality of opportunity, especially if profits are devoted to programs that provide low-income kids a greater opportunity at financial prosperity (McIntosh et al., 2020). The Annie E. Casey Foundation (2016) said that investment in people permits people to finance themselves which enables them to envision and self-confidently reach for chances for their families while simultaneously mitigating the economic hindrances that affect them. This would improve social stability by producing devoted proprietors and a labor force with the schooling and skill set needed for well-paid employment, helping the country's future progress. Helping improve the quality of life for these people translates to undoing decades of prejudicial policies and making positive gains, which calls for a mixture of tiny attainable stages and courageous vision.

Powell et al. (2019) explained that there is a thirst for new action and immediate policy changes that can disrupt the current deadlock and difficulties that prevent progress and generate innovative paths that would enable people and societies to flourish. In a period of political division and economic austerity, proposed solutions are either universal or targeted to a specific group. Universal solutions may be valid in a multicultural context but may be too grandiose and costly and not do enough to help the people greatest in need. Consequently, the marginalized and poor tend to regard universal policies with suspicion. Although policies targeted at a specific group may be more effective and less expensive, they may be perceived as favoring one group over another, causing anger and antipathy.

Targeted universalism entails setting explicit and universal goals and developing targeted policies or processes to achieve them (Powell et al., 2019). Targeted universalism discards an absolute universal which is expected to be tolerable to the actuality that dissimilar groups are positioned differently in comparative to the establishments and assets of society. Targeted universalism discards the assertion of formal equality that would regard all persons equally as a way of refuting difference. Any request would be assessed by the result, not just the intention. While the attempt would be universal for the poor, it would be specifically delicate to the most marginal groups (Perrius, 2011). This method takes account of the needs of specific groups, including powerful and influential or majority groups, and gaining the collaboration of everybody in terms of letting them know we are all together no matter what our social backgrounds may be. The five strategies for implementing targeted universalism are creating a universal goal grounded in a common or general appreciation of a societal problem and shared objectives, evaluating the action of the general populace in terms of the universal goal, recognizing groups that approach the goal in a different way, evaluating the structures and organizations that back each group or community or hinder it from attaining the universal goal, and developing and promoting targeted stratagems for each group to reach the universal goal (Powell et al., 2019).

Lifetime Investments from the Start

Ariel Investments founder and CEO, John Rogers explains, "We didn't have a grandfather or aunt or uncle or mom and dad educating us on the markets because they didn't benefit from it because of historical discrimination in this country," (Choe, 2020, para, 3). Blacks in most cases did not have the chance to create wealth, put it in the market and see it expand over the years. Usually, they have lesser earnings which amounts to less cash to invest once bills are paid. In addition, most who are employed do not have access to retirement plans. Scholars say that even better-off Black families are a lot less probable to possess stocks than whites, missing out on about 260% returns for S&P 500 funds over the past ten years (Choe, 2020).

The best way to grow one's money is over a period of time to gain compounding interest. (Compound interest will be discussed further and more explicitly in

Chapter 4). Therefore, saving money from the beginning of one's life through the end is imperative. Studies confirm that families with savings accounts are considerably more likely to gain a postsecondary education. As children grow older, they should develop their own investment behaviors by putting away money for unforeseen circumstances and building up long-term reserves for acquisitions like a house and opening retirement accounts that are financed in government investment bonds that eradicate the risk of losing principal. In addition, in terms of aid, the government can ensure that every young person has reserves by producing general savings accounts with start-up money deposits for newborn babies.

Restructure Government Policies

Government aid and policies to help people in need are effective, but simultaneously, they impede their progress by placing restrictions on benefits that discourage savings amongst these people. Prevented from being able to grow their earnings and savings, people will stay committed to their dependence on these programs. Government policy should encourage the people in these programs to determine how much they consume and how much they save in relation to their family income to help alleviate poverty and promote their well-being. While laws are in place on housing proprietorship by way of tax and policy, the less used possibility of aid such as the Government Housing and Urban Development's (HUD) voluntary Family Self-Sufficiency (FSS) program aids persons with housing vouchers to grow revenue, create moneys, and expand economic solidity (Asante-Muhammad et al., 2017).

> Perry and Romer, 2020, repeat Ashleigh Gardere, Senior Advisor to the president, PolicyLink who emphasizes, "DBE programs and small business training will never be enough to close the racial wealth gap in America—that's just tinkering at the edges. We need racial equity standards in the private sector: from greater access to capital beyond traditional debt to new and reparative financial products, from private sector business opportunities to narrative change strategies that center and celebrate Black businesses" (para 28).

MONEY HAS NO COMPLEXION

Asante-Muhammad et al. (2017) stated that there is a need to change the United States tax code to stop funding for the rich and instead aid funding for the poor, to modify the mortgage interest subtractions and tax expenses, and to extend the federal estate tax and protection for low-income housing from prosperity denudation procedures.

Furthermore, the states should play a sound role helping disadvantaged people save and become homeowners as well by cutting rapacious lending and making available 529 accounts and prize-connected savings. The individual states can put a lid on interest rates for loans and credit. In addition, states can create these aid accounts for each child and form affiliations with economic entities and other charities to help them grow (Annie E. Casey Foundation, 2016).

Many nations and empires have fallen throughout history for various reasons, but Noah Webster, American editor and writer in the 1700s noted, "The causes which destroyed the ancient republics were numerous; but in Rome, one principal cause was the vast inequality of fortunes" (Inequality.org, 2021, Quotes, para 12). The United States which has modeled many of its foundational rules on the Roman Empire may be headed towards the same fate as Rome.

Over five decades have passed since Dr. Martin Luther King's famous "I have a Dream" speech calling for civil and economic rights for Blacks and an end to racial discrimination, 10 decades after slavery officially ended. In his speech, Dr. King talked about segregation as well as the financial aspects of the Black society which he described as "living in the lonely island of poverty in the midst of a vast ocean of material prosperity" (p.25). Emphasizing this notion, he stressed that the nation had evaded its initial promise of opportunity for persons of color, mentioning checks to African Americans that had been refunded as having "insufficient funds." This example of racial financial inequality that he denounced continues in contemporary times (Asante-Muhammad et al., 2017).

The lasting obstacles to Black economic equality continue to be structural and not personal barriers. Those in authority in the United States are accountable for furthering this gap or helping to close it. It is up to the nation's leaders, government officials, politicians, and people to ensure that the gap shrinks or disappears. As with the Civil Rights Act and other laws that were put in place yet replaced by other discriminatory policies, the same will continue to occur if the people in control do not only change or fix these impeding policies but adapt and make them better while keeping them in place (Schermerhorn, 2019). American religious leader and editor of *Sojourners Magazine (1999)*, Jim Wallis, expressed his views on inequality in the United States and helping the poor, saying, "There's no more central theme in the Bible than the immorality of inequality. Jesus speaks more about the gap between rich and poor than he does about heaven and hell." (Inequality.org, 2021, Quotes, para 36).

Trina Edwards, Certified Professional Coach, MSN, and CEO of Diversity Recruitment Partners, explains shaping generational wealth like this:

> It wasn't until my youngest son, Chancellor, was a senior in high school that I realized our kids had actually been learning from my husband and me about healthy financial habits. I was astonished to learn that my son had signed up for an investing elective at school, and told him that I would not have thought in a million years that he had an interest in accounting and finance.
>
> My son replied, "I don't. I just want to learn how to become wealthy while I'm young enough to spend it and enjoy it." Was it possible that our kids were actually picking up the point that "money doesn't grow on trees"?
>
> Chancellor's interest ultimately became so strong that his teacher ended up mentoring him. This was an incredible opportunity for our son—after all, this teacher was a successful businessman who had recently entered the education field to share his investing insights. At the same time, I couldn't help but think, "Wow, I wish we had more Black wealth-preneurs who could come spread this knowledge in all of our communities."
>
> But it seems that, on a micro level, that's just what my husband, Preston, and I had done for our kids. I was happy to learn that Chancellor's seemingly newfound interest was actually sparked by his parents' work to grow our teacher recruitment magazine business.

Maybe, in this daily observation, our kids had a chance to see Preston and me not only as parents, but also as business partners who had different but shared experiences with how we learned about money. Preston grew up in a family business, which allowed him to learn money management and the importance of frugality firsthand. On my side, I watched my mother work for the U.S. government and take advantage of the Thrift Savings Plan for government workers. While the ways our parents earned money were different, the messages were the same: financial success came a little easier when you earn, budget, invest, and eliminate debt.

This sense of frugality did help us achieve some of our earlier goals, but if I'm being totally honest, the translation of yesterday's message into today's world sounds a lot like fear. How to fear money. How to live worrying it'll all be gone if we don't work, work, work and save, save, save.

Although our own parents are now retired and financially secure, my husband and I realize that if we want true financial freedom, we have to adjust our mindset. We agree that we will carry forward the lessons of very hard work and the values of integrity and honesty, but we've also learned that keeping frugality as our only focus actually prevents financial growth.

One way to ultimate financial wealth as a people is growing financially as a family. To do that, we must be willing to eliminate the fears we have associated with money. No more fear that drives us towards immediate gratification or validation in the form of consumerism, like designer clothes or cars. But we will also let go of the fear that we could "lose it all" at any moment and do nothing but save, save, save. By growing our mindset, by showing our kids the faith we had that investing in our business would grow our real wealth, maybe we helped them make the greatest investment of all.

At the end of his senior year, Chancellor started an investment club. During team dinners and weekly meetings in the gym, he would teach his friends and basketball teammates what he was learning in class.

Ironically, he had started doing exactly what I'd hoped someone out there would do. Not only was my son teaching peers who needed the lesson as much as he did, but my son also taught me a priceless lesson: you don't have to be rich to teach about wealth.

Many of us need to relearn what we were taught. We need to educate ourselves and each other on true facts about money, including how our own psychology can help us accumulate wealth. As entrepreneurs determined to achieve financial wealth, Preston and I are learning as we go and sharing these lessons. We now know that earning money means market penetration, that budgeting means taking a good look at our needs and our wants and knowing the difference between the two. We know that saving isn't just about a shoebox under the bed or a tired old checking account, but money market accounts and CDs, and diverse investing options.

The greatest investment of all lies in educating yourself and teaching your kids how to continue to educate themselves, so they can keep spreading the knowledge to their peers and community. This is how generational wealth is shaped.

We all know the old saying: If you teach the children how to fish, they will know how to fish. But, if you teach them where to fish and how to help others find more fish, the community will always have fish to eat and will never fear not having enough.

The Introduction along with Chapters 1 and 2 provided a comprehensive picture of the history of people of color, especially Blacks, emphasizing the income and wealth gap and its main causes. For people of color in the United States and the world to advance, action in the realms of societal reconstruction and education is imperative. Educating families about the need to be frugal and introducing basic information about investment and laws in schools may not close the gap entirely, or even much at all, but may prevent it from growing any bigger.

CHAPTER 3

MONEY CANNOT BUY HAPPINESS: BUT IT MAINTAINS A LIVING

As stated in Chapter 1, the wealth and income gap has had a profound effect on people of color and continues to do so. Only government legislation and the elected political figures and people in society can change that. Until then, people need to be frugal in their lifestyle, and the way to do so is to be aware of one's economic status while learning to make use of investments that suit one's means. Such sayings as do not write a check your rear end cannot cash, to make money you must have money, and stop trying to keep up with the Joneses are all well-known, and we all can relate to what they say about saving money and being frugal.

Success in life is about making choices and learning from them, realizing that each person is unique and has a different path in life. Therefore, to have any success with money and investing, being true and knowing oneself and not getting caught up in and being influenced by the media and commercial marketing is important, but it is easier said than done. To understand the trade-off of one's decisions, opportunity cost and the time value of money must be taken into consideration in relation to Maslow's pyramid as well as the importance of giving in various forms.

Opportunity Costs

In *Personal Finance: An Encyclopedia of Modern Money Management* (Friedberg, 2015), I wrote about opportunity cost in this manner, "opportunity cost is a fundamental economic concept. Opportunity cost involves making a choice between exclusive options about how to make use of a resource. In other words, opportunity cost involves the decision to give up one or more choices to accept a particular choice. This is generally a personal decision based on the perceptions of the person making the choice. The opportunity cost is then the other possible choices an individual could have made. The concept of opportunity cost is becoming more important in contemporary times as resources become scarcer and people become more aware of choices. Opportunity cost does not just involve financial expenditure alone but other activities in life as well. This means that it involves not only finances but also individual wants and needs, work and energy, as well as time. Once one understands the assets and liabilities of the potential decision, one may have a better idea what choice to make. It is important to comprehend both the direct expense of life and the indirect opportunity cost. Opportunity cost is in the eye of the beholder and depends on the given situation; the choices made will differ from person to person. One person may choose to obtain a college education for a certain dream and profession while another may not see the benefit in doing so due to the costs. When individuals evaluate and weigh the costs of different situations, they may come up with different results. As the world becomes more complex with resources becoming scarcer, the need to make sound decisions in all aspects of life will be crucial for individuals, societies, nations, and the world. As technology grows along with education and communication throughout the world is faster than in the past, the importance of sound thinking in life's decision-making process is crucial for all people. Yes, financial aspects including economically frugal decisions are a key to success in life, but then so is comprehending the value of money" (p. 176-179).

Time Value of Money

Many say that money is the root of all evil. Such may be the case, but I view this perception differently in saying that the love of money is a root of all kinds of evil. "Some people, eager for money, have wandered from the faith and pierced themselves with many griefs" (1 Timothy 6:10). This will be discussed later in terms of philanthropy and helping others. Nonetheless, money does have value and its worth does change according to when and how one uses it.

Time value of money can be described as forthcoming money equivalent to current money when time is added. In simple lay terms, a greenback was of more value yesterday than today and a buck today is valued more than a buck tomorrow. This is factual because money that one may consume currently can be invested and earn a return, consequently generating a greater sum in the future. One must take into consideration that with imminent cash, further risk can occur in terms of receiving future cash for various reasons.

How to make choices in line with one's values can free up needed and wanted money in terms of saving and investing for tomorrow. Values and choices differ from person to person and culture to culture, domestically as well as globally, causing a debate about present and future economic stability, as was noted in Chapter 1. Nonetheless, impressing others is a waste of time, and in many cases, a waste of money.

Making the choice to give up a lot of stuff and reclaiming a life of purpose and contentment is a key aspect of achieving financial security. One must figure out how to decide how much stuff is enough and how to free up more money to live the life one really wants and buy the important things. Buying unneeded stuff leads to short-lived happiness, but conscious spending can lead to both spiritual and financial wealth. Identifying what's important guides one to live a more meaningful life and become richer.

Johnson (2020) cited a story distributed by the Nielsen Company entitled "It's in the Bag: Black Consumers' Path to Purchase" that claimed that spending by Black consumers is particularly influenced by advertising. The article claimed that Black people enjoy spending money on beauty and grooming goods and at top-quality stores. African Americans are more influenced than others by store staff, advertising, and merchandising. Black people accounted for virtually 90% of the total expenditure in the beauty supply industry. In addition, Blacks tend to be influenced by personalities and are more likely to purchase a product or service promoted by a celebrity.

> Nielson, 2015 states, "Brands often use celebrities to boost the appeal of their products or services to potential consumers. Celebrities have qualities that can be both aspirational and relatable, and marketers depend on these strong attributes to gain consumers' trust and brand loyalty. For African American consumers, celebrity endorsements have

purchase implications across all income levels, but the connection is the strongest among households earning $50,000-$75,000, who are 96% more likely than non-Hispanic White counterparts to consider making a purchase if that product or service is endorsed by a celebrity" (para 3).

Johnson (2020) cited Senior Vice President Cheryl Grace as saying that research shows that Black customer selections are influenced by a "cool factor" that encourages not only customers of color but the majority to purchase certain items. Statistics prove that money spent by multinational conglomerates on researching and developing products and marketing that attracts diverse customers is certainly worth their while. Reed (2017) quoted a report saying Black purchasing power is presently $1.3 trillion. With this amount of cash, Black's ought to be employing procedures that put those greenbacks into Black enterprises. To achieve equality in the United States society, Blacks must study how to shape business and investments, hold onto them, and pass them on to future generations. Alcorn (2021) explained that the social undertaking to back Black-owned banks and other African American entities was enhanced as a result of George Floyd's slaying on May 25, 2020, as business and corporate leaders as well as ordinary United States citizens looked for opportunities to discuss long-standing socioeconomic inequalities between Black and White United States citizens. With this type of participation which is a good example of the general systems theory and interactive social system working at their best, the closing of the huge gap between Blacks and Whites has a chance to happen. The help of people from all walks of life as well as people of color making the right choices in terms of their finances can create opportunities for investment. Understanding one's essential needs is the first step in doing so.

Financing is simply managing money and assets so that a person or organization can focus on making a profit while curtailing risks and losses. The action can involve such facets as saving, lending, budgeting, investing, borrowing, and predicting the future. In doing so, they need to know about the organization and estimate whether they can make use of the proper type of financing, such as equity or debt financing, which will be discussed in Chapter 7.

Business financing is a broad term with many different facets. Personal financing involves individuals in terms of their own finances. A great personal finance book or encyclopedia to read for overall knowledge with examples would be *Personal Finance: An Encyclopedia of Modern Money Management* (Friedberg, 2015). Corporate finance and government and public finance are other common general aspects of financing. In this book, the emphasis will be on personal finance and being frugal so that some level of wealth can be acquired.

Frugalness

For many, a frugal lifestyle is the way to overall well-being and improving their financial situation. After the Great Recession, people were presented with the idea of using a pennywise financial plan. This plan permitted them to reduce their expenditures so that additional money became available to them. These extra funds were then utilized to help reform their devastated economic lives.

Food is a need, but if one is frugal, one will consume more meals at home because this reduces this specific expenditure. Therefore, the first step to a frugal life is to work out one's needs and wants, with more emphasis on the former than on than the latter.

It is hard to be frugal if one cannot determine what needs and wants are. Frugality is not about dispossessing oneself, or being parsimonious, and if viewed and practiced in the right way, one can be rewarded and relish what one loves to do and simultaneously create savings. Prudence is recognizing what is essential and what is not. Necessities are the aspects of life that one must have like food and water, shelter, clothing, and health maintenance while wants to pertain to the nonessentials one partakes in that one can survive without. A frugal consumer is typically hard to influence and invulnerable to a degree to peer pressure. Nonetheless, when one is with associates and relatives who spend unreasonably, one may be inclined to partake in impulsive spending as well. This is why one must be careful in terms of living a frugal life (National Debt Relief, 2016).

Understanding one's personal needs can at times cause conflicts in terms of priority and choice. Companies undertake extensive research to understand not only consumers' needs but also their wants. One's wants can be the main obstacle to being frugal in terms of saving. People need physiological requirements, safety, love and belonging, esteem, and self-actualization. Starting with the most important to Maslow, let us see how these needs fit into one's life in terms of finance and investment.

Maslow's Pyramid

Basic Needs: Physiological and Safety

According to the Nielson report, food is also another shopping sector that Black folks spend liberally on. According to Nielsen's report, "soul food" is a major driver for "African American consumers' top grocery purchases," including certain brands like "Quaker grits ($19 million); Louisiana Fish Fry ($11 million); Glory Greens (frozen and fresh, $9.5 million combined) and Jay's Potato Chips (nearly $2.7 million)" (Wright, 2020, para 7).

We all need food, water, warmth, and rest. No matter what we do in life, these are a daily part of our existence. However, our choice of food and drink has a profound impact on both our finances and our health. A difficulty in obtaining food and drink is that in some demographic areas, healthy food may not be as easily obtainable, and if it is, the cost is usually high. Nonetheless, one still can make wise choices in terms food and drink and savings.

MONEY HAS NO COMPLEXION

Remember that what one puts into one's body not only costs money but may also cost one one's well-being or life in the long run. So, consider frugal spending a life saver, literally! One may want to consider the way of thinking that I call the mind, body, and spirit concept. One can learn to be frugal with all three of these aspects, starting with the inner spirit that makes the mind and body function properly. I have found in life that if I try to function with the mind or body first, then nothing works out. But when I focus on the spirit first and let it take the lead, then the mind and body can operate effectively and efficiently. Being frugal with the spirit means not over thinking or doing, just having appropriate faith, patience, and discipline in the spirit. In doing so, a frugal mind and body will follow.

Not only are food and drink essential for our physiological well-being, but so is the necessity to keep warm which includes clothing and shelter. As stated earlier in this chapter, clothing is something that people pay too much for, and whether they realize it or not, it can be a "waste" of money. Instead of just acquiring basic clothing for one's needs, many indulge in purchasing high-end brands. I would be a hypocrite to say that that does not include me, and many who read this book will agree. Along with physiological needs, psychological needs and self-fulfillment are also in Maslow's hierarchy, and clothing can also fall into these categories. Besides comfort and warmth, clothing can give one a sense of being accepted or even self-awareness. Therefore, the price to pay for these aspects can be a major factor.

Instead of purchasing expensive name-brand clothing, it is highly recommended to buy apparel that is cost effective. In addition, the media and commercialization add to this perception, placing subconscious pressure on people to go out and spend to meet their need for self-fulfillment.

Remember opportunity cost? The trade-off is high: pricey clothing or money invested in a future and assets that can make one live comfortably with the ability to give to others. Faith, patience and discipline! Instead of going to the mall or expensive clothing stores, go to secondhand stores such as the Salvation Army, Good Will, or other "Hand Me Down" places. Yes, it may sound "beneath" one, but one would be surprised what these clothing places have. For example, one can try going to a Salvation Army or Good Will in a wealthy neighborhood. One person's trash is another's treasure! In addition, one can hit two birds with one stone by giving to the Salvation Army or Good Will and in return, find frugal clothing that suits one's means. Trust me! You will be surprised what is in these stores. Take the clothes home, wash them, and nobody will know the difference.

Like clothing, transportation and housing are also major facets that may involve high costs and can also be considered a poor investment. As we learned from Chapters 1 and 2, the income and wealth gap continues to affect people of color tremendously. Even if one wants a nice expensive house and car, the ability to acquire them is out of reach due to lack of funds. Having said that, with credit availability and other loaning opportunities, especially with automobiles, the opportunity presents itself. A car is one of the worst investments that one can make because the value drops (depreciation) as soon as one pays for it and drives it off the car lot.

Buying a house can be a positive, but having enough money to finance it, maintaining the payments, and keeping up with the maintenance are the usual downfalls of house owners. Furthermore, many do not have the know-how or discipline to personally finance their funds, causing them to live beyond their means.

Dr. Scena Webb, a motivated and knowledgeable educator, Navy veteran, author, entrepreneur, and servant leader, shares from the heart her insights on building wealth based on her vast life experience. Before buying anything, she believes it is important to give (to a shelter and her church). She heeds the 80/20 rule, emphasizing living on 20% of her and her husband's acquired income and giving the rest away. She used to believe in tithing ($200 weekly) but soon understood that tithing was more than the monetary aspects. In addition, she ascertained and experienced that giving required the first fruits (her best) which included her gifts of teaching and advising students and people of all walks of life. Action is important to Dr. Scena, and abilities, which are unique gifts from God, are a true part of tithing. She says, "Our own personal stories are not for us to keep to ourselves, but to share to the world and tie them in the hearts and minds of various diverse people throughout the world. The tithing of time and action are what it is all about, not just monetary input."

In terms of investing, Dr. Scena emphasizes that investing is in the eye of the beholder and that she does not invest more than $500 on a single stock and that

$200 is ideal. She has developed these frugal ideas since childhood when she experienced the Ken and Barbie doll mindset early about matching clothes and being thrifty in doing so. Purchasing only what she likes and investing in that product is key:

> I like Tide detergent, Amazon, Walmart, and other products and services. Therefore, I invest in them! In doing so, I pay myself back from purchasing these items. Look around your house and see what you buy and invest in it. Don't just be a consumer purchasing what others say to buy; buy what you use and invest in it. These actions will result in paying yourself back. Look in your closet, in the fridge, and invest in what you buy and have. Spend money and let it cycle back to you! And remember! Money is a tool to do things if used appropriately and wisely! My last investment was Pfizer; once the pandemic happened, I asked many people which shot they acquired, and they said Pfizer. Therefore, I invested, and the rest is history!

Psychological: Belonging, Love, and Esteem

The introduction of this book explained the importance of the general systems theory (not being alone) and interactive social system (working together) and the relationship between them, and this relates to Maslow's pyramid in terms of how one needs to have intimate relationships and friends. What was discussed above in the physiological needs section of the pyramid holds true here with the sense of belonging, love, and esteem. In terms of personal relationships, many may find it necessary to spend a lot to please others and themselves. Love is a broad concept and can make one go through tremendous feats to please others or oneself, creating happiness for oneself or others and a feeling of prestige or accomplishment at a high monetary cost.

The title of this chapter is Money Cannot Buy Happiness. Such may be the case in terms of self- fulfillment and achieving one's full potential. From my personal perception and life experiences along with the experiences of many others, I have found that true and appropriate love is the key to happiness. Many in life seek to fulfill their potential or dreams, but once the accomplishment is attained, it wears off and the cycle of need for fulfillment goes on. In doing so, much time and money is spent, and until the person no longer has the funds or realizes what happiness is, this cycle continues.

Education has always been an important topic. The discussion of the income and wealth gap in this book has made it clear that one's chances of succeeding in life are slim unless one is blessed with a talent that one can develop and make use of. The numbers show that it is better to have education and the more, the better, but even with education (even with a doctorate, the highest academic degree), a job or position that pays accordingly is still hard to find.

Therefore, the money spent over the years in terms of opportunity cost may not be worth the benefit cost analysis especially if a student loan has been taken out. As a matter of fact, one may be in deeper debt than one was before entering college, creating an even wider gap in income and wealth among people of color. Having money to pay for education and using student loans are two separate issues. One can imagine, if one had the knowledge, discipline, and confidence to do so, that if the opportunity presented itself to work at a simple job such as a fast-food chain, one could make appropriate investments and save up for the future so that some level of wealth can be acquired. This is true not just in the United States, but globally as well.

Jane Kasumba, broadcaster, lawyer, entrepreneur, and investor, states that

> before making an investment of any kind, one must do research to learn how the investment has performed in the past and currently and its projections for the future. One should make a point of conferring with specialists in one's preferred discipline and legal advisers who may be able to assist one. One must also familiarize oneself with the regulations that oversee the region in which the investment will be made. When making a foreign investment, ensure the procedures that one is going through are legal and will produce the anticipated results. One should continually attempt to use the government's guiding principles so that one can be safeguarded and profit from incentives for investors.

MONEY HAS NO COMPLEXION

After observing the statistical data about contemporary and imminent forecasts on several internet sites, there is no doubt in my mind, that Africa is the neoteric frontier in terms of investment prospects for one who is looking for a reasonable return on investment. The Africa Continental Free Trade Area (ACFTA) will generate the prime trading alliance in the world since the inception of the World Trade Organization (WTO). Africa has a young and energetic population, immense raw materials, and a profusion of mineral wealth.

The African Union (AU) and its associate states are making investment in the continent a matter of importance. As a result, there is a concentrated energy by the AU to warrant diplomatic and socioeconomic amalgamation of the continent, endorse and secure African mutual opinions on issues of interest to the continent and its people, and to encourage intercontinental collaboration. An investor arriving in Africa nowadays will realize the continent is fixated on the progress of innovative segments such as telecommunications, tourism, consumption, and infrastructure.

The continent is also going through a population explosion with the population anticipated to grow two-fold in the next 30 years, then attaining 4.3 billion people by the year 2100 to tally for 40% of the world's inhabitants. Africans will offer a youthful active labor force with the ability to utterly alter the continent. Presently, Africa's market capitalization to GDP is the lowest in the world, and investors are likely to profit from capital market progress in the coming years. Africa's constant acclimatization to technology and internet management has seen many technology titans acquire an interest in the continent, with several of them investing in Africa to profit from the youthful labor force. Africa is an enormous continent, with immense infrastructural needs. This poses an irreplaceable prospect for investors in the infrastructural area to unearth and invest in enterprises that will promise an enhanced and united Africa. Africa is swiftly adjusting to and acting in opposition to climate change. The continent is now looking for investors who will generate eco-friendly enterprises. This provides a substantial chance for investors in this arena. Africa is on the identical progress course as was seen in the rise of the Asian Tigers. It will not be long before it sees a sustained decrease in poverty and growth in all areas. The prospects in Africa will not persist as virgin eternally. Investors in this new frontier will secure a return on their investment.

See you in Africa!

Yes, in many cases, those who do have low-wage employment barely get by or cannot make a living with the wages that they earned, and this continues to be a dilemma as we saw in the earlier chapters. Until legislation is passed in terms of employment and wages as well as in other situations, investing is easier said than done. But it is possible! Everyone should remember always to vote at every election at all levels!

The key is to have an ideal reasonable path to success, which will differ from person to person. Remember! Once your personal finance and investing begins and grows, always give back! I would have this in Maslow's pyramid if I could because one way of obtaining one's needs is the gesture of giving, whether one gives money or service. Many may disagree, but I know from experience that it is true.

Philanthropy: Give No Matter What

A study from 2012, (Black Americans donate to make a difference | Reuters), discovered that African Americans give a greater share of their revenue to charitable foundations than any other group in the country (Wright, 2020). Tracey Webb, founder of Washington D.C-based Black Benefactors, previously told NewsOne. *"From our communities in Africa to the Underground Railroad and the Civil Rights Movement, Black collective giving is something that's inherent in us." (para 2).*

Colossal progress from 1500-1750 altered the way people lived and positioned themselves in global affairs. As the old world declined, so did its economic, political, and social institutions. Conflicts and revolution led to the downfall of the feudal system which defined common responsibilities between property-owner and laborer. Mediaeval aristocrats no longer protected the well-being of their dependents, which released peasants from their obligation to stay and work for their masters.

Currently, philanthropists work to advance and fortify societies, fund the arts, shape institutes, increase educational ideals, fight disease, and deliver reprieve for the victims of war and natural tragedies in a myriad of ways. They make contributions and agree to help local and worldwide developments. Philanthropic foundations fund research, and firms support their communities through corporate social responsibility programs. In addition, technology has allowed prompt, worldwide interactions, and charity has flourished in the technological milieu, resulting in new ways to help and empower those in need and allow them to participate in their upliftment (National Philanthropic Trust, 2016).

As one can see, philanthropy has evolved over time, and people give for many reasons. For example, there are numerous boards across the United States and the world that are designed to demonstrate philanthropic action. In many cases, these boards are not giving because they care, but the action is to make the entity that they represent look good providing them with an outward appearance of generosity. Furthermore, many entities that seek to provide help to others hurt the recipients by their actions.

> Perry and Romer, 2020 repeat Stephen Deberry, Founder and Chief Investment Officer at Bronze Investments, "We know large corporates and others have publicly committed many billions to support Black businesses and communities, but most of them aren't organically connected to Black people or places. The best way to leverage those is to invest in Black-led financial firms with a history and strategy to invest in high growth business led by Black people. This is the delicious low-hanging fruit of U.S. economic recovery" (para 16).

Doctoral candidate, Ron Hoggard, entrepreneur, nonprofit owner, and conversant investor, shares his story:

> The most telling instance of image repair is in the case of a certain well-known corporation one shall call Corporation X with their mission.

Around 2013, Corporation X needed a social image revamp based on their involvement in several scandals. Transgressions included the London whale trading scandal, their involvement in the acquisition of two banks which sold bad mortgages during the Great Recession, failing to spot the Ponzi scheme activities of Bernie Madoff, and countless other misdeeds. The initiative Corporation X started with was the financial rescue of the city of Detroit, Michigan; advancing cities came later. The plan was to rescue the recently bankrupt city from what seemed like a hopeless situation. Seeing that Detroit was once a bustling metropolis and the fastest growing city which fell from grace, corporate generosity was the city's saving grace.

The interest in helping the city came as a welcome gesture according to a prominent city official. The investment would help the city with resources such as running buses and working light fixtures. Corporation X would also provide home loans to citizens, provide resources to rebuild dilapidated buildings in the downtown and Mid-town areas, and make grants to small businesses effecting change in the community. The large financial investment could seemingly provide the city with the necessary assets to pull itself out of financial restraint. The only issue was that most of the citizens of Detroit recognize a glass ceiling which prohibits them from access to donors and benevolence efforts. Where philanthropy hurt Detroit was the general understanding that the urban areas were being gentrified for the profit of kept groups. The working-class residents did not have an opportunity to gain the lion's share of generosity because of the effects of targeted philanthropy.

Where this philanthropic effort was mismanaged is in the development of a strategy which is directly linked with community leaders and social activist groups. Corporation X may have cared about where its money was going, but the citizens asked for results and have only been bombarded with promises. Residents in Detroit see something happening, but those opportunities are not readily available for groups outside of a specific social circle. Citizens know the buildings which are being rehabbed would not be sold to a community activist group

MONEY HAS NO COMPLEXION

or a middle-class resident because they are owned by philanthropic organizations themselves. So, when an entity such as Corporation X comes along with benevolence at the core of its strategy, it can be considered a donation from, and in many cases, to the controlling hands of wealth. In essence the wealth is only distributed at the top of the social ladder. Many families' net of financial prosperity and preservation is casted wider due to these actions. Meanwhile in the poverty-stricken areas of Detroit, citizens are forced into deeper need thus lowering their chance of a fair generational wealth outcome.

Philanthropy can improve corporations' social image in the initial stages, but the results are often disappointing. In philanthropy, the misuse of benevolence in association with governmental benefits provides an uneven surface for America. Philanthropists are largely unregulated which leads to ideologies such as philanthrocapitalism. In this theory, commodities are exchanged with philanthropic endeavors to dodge tax repercussions and preserve wealth. This lack of ordinance has gotten so much attention in recent years because of the efforts of the world's wealthiest families and their donations to charity. The unwritten understanding is wealth can be transferred with less capital gains and estate taxes if donations are given to charity. Some of these charities are owned by the donor. In the large view, philanthrocapitalism is here to stay with large donors such as Bill and Melinda Gates, Jeff Bezos, and Mark Zuckerberg reaping the benefits based on the lack of regulation.

Carlozo, 2012 states that African American contributors donate a greater portion of their earnings than white contributors according to an analysis. Although this is the case, they do not perceive themselves as huge beings in the charitable ring, and that displays a persona dilemma, explains experts such as Judy Belk, a senior vice president for Rockefeller Philanthropy Advisors. "African Americans have been very uncomfortable with the title of philanthropist," Belk said. "If you don't see role models who look like you when people start talking about issues related to philanthropy, you start believing, 'Hey, maybe I'm not a philanthropist" (para 1). Belk said she got so tired of this mindset and therefore created a 12-minute clip called, "I Am A Philanthropist," which features diverse faces, races and ethnicities of donors and grant-makers (para 1).

One may also ask how one can be frugal and save to invest and give at the same time. As we read, Dr. Scena Webb emphasized what true giving from the heart is, and the return-on-investment is the true gratification (Maslow's self-fulfillment and psychological needs) one receives. When giving comes from the heart, one can think of many ways to help others besides giving money. Labor, talents, skills, and time are in most cases better than money and needed tremendously. One can also volunteer and give away one's old or unused "stuff." One may think that old possessions are not wanted, but one person's trash is another person's treasure. One needed and often forgotten way to give is to pray for and with others. You would be amazed how that truly helps, and research proves such is the case. And remember Matthew 6:19-21 says, "Do not lay up for yourselves treasures on earth, where moth and rust destroy and where thieves break in and steal, but lay up for yourselves treasures in heaven, where neither moth nor rust destroys and where thieves do not break in and steal. For where your treasure is, there your heart will be also." Always give, people! Take heed and recollect that cash and assets are not the most important facets in life, but when utilized astutely, which includes sustaining oneself and one's household, as well as the needy, then money will be a valuable means.

Nevertheless, one should understand one's money and assets and not let these aspects regulate one's own life, keeping in mind that being thankful for what one has is more important than the amount that one can get. Give in all forms whether the generosity is in the form of money, assets, or time. When you give, make sure it is sincerely from the heart, not for attention and adulation, and do not look for something in return as if the giving is a business transaction.

Gregory Schwabe, Disabled Veteran and Former Assistant Special Agent of Counter-Intelligence in Korea, Actor, Executive Producer and Co-Creator of the Mini T.V. Series Buffalo Rangers and Executive Producer of Heroes From Heaven The Movie explains his journey and reason for giving.

So, to me it's funny to be talking about money and investing because for the longest time while in the United States Army I lived month to month, often with a negative ending balance each month. Money and investing were never a topic I sought information about or spoke about with my parents. But what I can say is that over the years I have put into practice several ideals that have allowed me to be more present in the world we live in and to create a more secure future. I remember a conscious decision I made in and around the 4th year of my military service. I realized I was never able to vacation or see my environment, because I was always broke. Then I calculated how much I spent on the weekends partying or eating out. I slowly stopped spending on the weekend and putting that money into a savings account titled travel, and the first year alone I was able to visit Thailand and the Philippines while stationed in Korea. I was saving 140 dollars a week by not going out. I also made another non-financial decision and that was to get rid of my TV. So, I was kind of forced to go out and explore. Bing watching TV was destroying my ability or desire to explore the world we live in. So those two life decisions allowed me to visit cities, countries, museums, and interact with people while saving money. I have been able to see and touch and smell and experience history and this amazing world we live in. That is far more important and fulfilling that wasting money on parties in my mind.

I also started investments with Acorns, several years ago, where transactions on my debit card are rounded up and invested into stocks. Over time I started using professionals to help manage investments for me. As an executive producer now of TV and movie projects, money is no longer a major issue, but I still look for ways to make my money work for me and to increase revenue streams. I remain quite frugal because of my family principles and my military service.

The other thing is as a Christian, I tithe 10 percent of what I make to my church and find other opportunities to help individuals, communities, or organizations in need of help. I don't expect anything in return, but I can honestly say that by giving I definitely get more in return. Many people partake in giving to get something back. They are actually using people or an organization to help their political aspirations and have turned their gesture of giving into a business deal and thus expect a return. It is true that money cannot buy happiness as one can see from the unhappiness at the deaths of people like entertainers, politicians, and athletes. Perhaps, this is because they did not fully comprehend the reason they are here and the importance of stewardship.

CHAPTER 4

THE FIERCE AND FEARLESS PATH TO FINANCIAL SUCCESS

Saving and Sound Budgeting

Modest financial attainment is described as the accomplishment of one's individual financial objectives. This refers to the objectives individuals make for themselves and not those determined by the social order. Studies show that once one makes a specified amount of cash, one's contentment does not increase a lot. So, truthfully, one can have achievement without a tremendous amount of cash. Budgetary accomplishment is more about intangible assets than earning enormous wealth.

Modest financial achievement not only signifies an assured tomorrow but also can provide one sufficient means to cover one's essential living expenses for the future. The amount of money one has will differ depending on where one resides and on one's way of life. One needs to decide one's main concerns and needs in terms of financial success and then develop one's financial behaviors.

The steps to financial liberty involve one's actions over time that will achieve one's objective. This means, first of all, living a simple life concentrating on the need for a home, transportation, and food. Contingent upon one's way of life, financial success does not have to mean having a lot of money, but one has to sort out what truly is of importance in life. If one does not have time to enjoy life, no matter how much money one has, one cannot genuinely relish financial success. The equation is simple but calls for proper planning and discipline. Make more and consume less; do not delay in investing and financial planning; and avoid borrowing money (Friedberg, 2021a).

Building a Foundation for Financial Success

Nitara Lee Osbourne, writer and business owner, writes this section:

I spent a good part of my adult life believing once "I make my millions," I can subscribe to the triad financial philosophy:

- Budget
- Save
- Invest

But the truth is that most people in the United States with some sort of income (poor and middle class included) can start exactly where they are to get where they want to be financially. You don't wait on success before you decide to do what successful people do. Action precedes the goal. Although America is far from perfect, it is one of few countries where you can start with nearly nothing and make a dream and vision into something tangible based upon desire, work, a willingness to learn, a plan, and persistence.

Most people can:

- Budget with the money they are currently earning.
- Save a comfortable percentage of what they bring in at any given time.
- Place a comfortable percentage of their income into an investment account so that when they are ready to invest, they have the means to do so without it interfering with income they need to pay current expenses. And for those who have access to a 401(k) through their employer, this opens up another opportunity to grow money for retirement.

The above list is what I subscribe to.

Learn how to budget, save, and invest from books and individuals who do all three effectively and successfully. And please be sure to consult a professional to provide you with financial guidance that makes sense for you and your situation.

What My Foundation Looks Like

I started late in the game when it came to budgeting, saving, and investing. While I wouldn't call myself frugal, I avoid spending money I don't have while still enjoying my life. In other words, I don't create new debts, but a portion of my income is dedicated to experiences or things that bring me joy. Being financially responsible doesn't mean being miserable. At this point, I have created three active income streams: (1) my job, (2) my ghostwriting and editing business, and (3) getting hired to write scripts and treatments as an independent contractor in the film industry. Passive income streams are next on my agenda, but let's focus on the active income for now.

Job

My full-time job is writing as a content specialist in the marketing department for a nationwide company that helps those struggling with substance misuse to get treatment. I love the work because I get to use my talents as a writer to contribute to a company with a powerful mission. That income allows me to donate to causes I care about, help people in my family, contribute to the company 401(k) plan, add to my investment account, pay my bills, and save.

Business

I also own a business and happily had to hire three independent contractors to supplement my own efforts based on the growth we had during the pandemic. The Infinite Writer Agency, LLC, allows me to help clients to create/edit their self-help manuscripts into book form, helps independent contractors to make money doing what they love, and finally, my company helps me to save and supplement my income. Owning a business can be an option as long as you (1) find a need and market (or create the need/market) and (2) you have the talent and/or acquired skills to deliver to that market. Although the ups and downs of business can be frustrating, it's empowering to have another income stream available.

Independent Contractor

Working as an independent contractor in the film industry is a rewarding endeavor for me as well. I love writing scripts! Having a producer hire me to write a treatment for a movie script or to write an adaptation of a script is the epitome of my dream as a writer. Although this income can be inconsistent, it's welcomed and appreciated just the same. I place that income into my savings or investment account to supplement my income when needed.

I write my own original scripts both for fun and with the intention of selling them or using them as writing samples to obtain for further screenwriting opportunities. And honestly, writing scripts while drinking my favorite drink (matcha green tea latte with soy) is my idea of happiness. Whatever you do in this life to create income, aim to be in your ultimate happy place as often as possible.

Some of the main elements of financial success include earning more, budgeting, saving, eliminating debt, and investing. These concepts are interrelated and include the trade-offs between spending and investing. Budgeting is important, and one should plan soundly, including a balance between one's personal savings and taking care of debt. The importance of paying off debt while simultaneously saving money is the key to financial success. In doing so, one's debt including interest rates and credit score can improve, and along with this mindset, one's saving can have a future impact on developing interest in terms of savings (compound interest) as well as having spare money, which will be discussed later.

The general equation that one may use is as follows: Take one's expenses (variable and fixed) and subtract them from one's monthly income. To get an idea of consistency, one can look at the result of the fixed and variable expenses minus income for a couple months and get a ballpark figure of what one's expenses are. This will provide an overall idea of one's spending and help one to live within one's means. One must make sure one is true to oneself in obtaining a general concept of what money is needed and at the same time, give oneself some leeway in terms of needing more money than what one states on the budget. Never assume the money included (income tax, financial support, or assumed cash) is definite. Also, one should be true to oneself in eliminating unneeded expenses or purchasing nonessentials. Moreover, it is imperative to avoid impulse buying and extra fees like bank and late fees and to use cash when available as well as debit transactions if need be.

Retired veteran (United States Marine) Don Bradley says that many people want their cash to multiply but do not have the discipline or know-how for it to do so. People want to be successful in these economically challenging times, but many do not understand how to make use of money in terms of being frugal and making good investment choices. To be economically prudent, one needs first to respect one's money and honor it as an essential part of one's well-being.

Respecting money requires self-restraint and planning. Crafting a budget will provide a better picture and aid in ascertaining one's financial needs and expenditures, which in turn generates a habit of fundamental money management. This does not require an accounting or finance degree, but the simple notion of knowing your assets and liabilities including your debit and credit information (savings, household bills, car payments, insurance, food (not fast food), credit card payments, student loans etc.). Once the liabilities are subtracted from the assets, what is left can be put into savings and or invested. Yes, due to the wealth and income gap, many do not have much to save or even a thought to invest due to having no inherited wealth and their employment situations, but any little bit over time counts. Each person's economic condition will differ but the same holds true in being frugal: Patience and discipline!

Many think that frugalness implies being cheap, stingy, or tight with money. In all reality, frugal people understand and respect money and therefore are conscious of how they spend their money by doing things like using coupons and looking for sales and discounts. The object is to pay for quality products and services at a lower cost while retaining as much money as possible.

When one gains respect for money, then one has a better chance of procuring the benefits of consuming it. Besides inheriting money, the wealthy and affluent secure additional assets because they respect money and grasp how it operates.

Finally, one should make sure that one comprehends how to make money work in a positive way while by using money or asset opportunities that fit one's abilities. This can be ensured by way proper investments in sound, legal, and good-quality money making activities such as investing in the stock market or real estate or owning a business or other investment that will increase in value or provide a positive cash return.

Compound Returns

Compound returns can convert a percentage of one's lifetime earnings into even more money. Albert Einstein called compound interest "the most powerful force in the universe" and said, "He who understands it earns it. He who does not pays it." Billionaire Warren Buffett said, "My wealth has come from a combination of living in America, some lucky genes, and compound interest. I always knew I was going to be rich, so I was never in a hurry." Benjamin Franklin described it as "Money makes money. And the money that money makes, makes money" (Sather, 2021, p. 1).

Good things come to those that wait! Patience, discipline ... is the key. I always say to myself in terms of teaching and learning, KEEP IT SIMPLE Stupid! The same holds true in investing. Investing is good if one has the know-how even if one is unfortunate, impecunious, or inexperienced. Sather (2021) says time is of the essence, and the sooner one comprehends this in terms of finance and investing, the better off they will be. Opportunity cost involves a trade-off which includes being bored and impatient. But in the long run, it pays off and expands big time. Sather states that compounding interest is patience. The results are not instantaneous and can be somewhat tedious. Compounding interest is a prodigious counterbalance. It works by momentum, and it can turn ordinary people into tycoons. It teaches patience and discipline, lets one sleep well at night, is the friend of the underprivileged, separates the rich from the destitute, and can save the future for the next generation.

> Tilbury, 2011, explains that, "GROWING a bank balance from zero to $10,000 in just one year or building a big nest egg over decades does not require any big risk-taking. It's simply about watching your spending and then reinvesting your money. If you can learn this lesson early in life and learn to appreciate and love the power of compound interest, it›s likely you›ll have more money than your friends ever will. The bottom line is you need to be tight and not spend your money on stupid things. Remember this mantra: If it does you no good in the future, don›t buy it" (para 1).

Compounding interest is not concerned about race, gender, or age. Compounding interest touches everybody the same because it is contingent on time. Many older people will say that time in terms of life is of the essence and they would like to have more time. Sather (2021) compares compound interest to an avalanche, saying powerful natural phenomena have small beginnings. For example, a little snow gathers more snow that is compacted with great force and eventually becomes an avalanche. When the snowball is gathered, it rolls downhill, by the force of its own momentum. One's wealth operates just like the snowball. The work one must do at the start is often stressful and can be mentally consuming. But when the snowball (wealth) starts to accumulate, it entices more snow (wealth entices more wealth). This is when compound interest is working in the service of the investor (Sather, 2021). Remember! Patience, discipline, know-how, and the right choices are the key! Many make excuses, saying that they do not have the cash to participate in the stock market, but honestly, you do not need a lot of cash to do so. This is what compounding interest does. Putting your money into entities that are growing means more dollars are distributed to stockholders which means a starting investment can reproduce in the long run, an idea that should not be undervalued. "We learn about compound interest at secondary school, but we forget it. We shouldn't. Einstein is quoted (probably apocryphally) as describing it as ``the greatest mathematical discovery of all time" (Dunn, n.d., para 9)

Compound interest is utilized best with conventional investing. One should not pursue questionable trends but stay neutral from month to month. Look for those entities that are growing constantly, gradually, and assuredly. Remember the story of the hare and the turtle! The turtle wins in the end. The wealthy smile every day in most cases due to knowing that they are compounding money as we speak. Time and patience are money! One can use an approach called dollar cost averaging which is soundly operative since it instills discipline paradigms and sound behaviors but also stops one from suffering unneeded mishaps in the stock market. One must comprehend that trying to time the stock market is ludicrous. The market is enormous, transferring trillions of bucks a second in and out of securities, futures, and commodities. One cannot estimate what the market will do in the future. And if one is seeking advice from professionals, good luck! Sometimes, it works, but in many cases it does not. I like to say that the days of the prophets in terms of EXACT FORETELLING ARE LONG OVER. Not to say that these experts know nothing, but as I always say to myself in terms of learning and teaching, keep it simple stupid! Sather (2021) says that dollar cost averaging is a sound way to invest. Investing the same amount of cash in the stock market each month results in buying a smaller amount when the stock market is up and purchasing extra when the market is down. In other words, buy low and sell high! Therefore, do not be avaricious and follow others. For instance, enormous interest credit due does not go down when you make a payment. The high interest debt hurts one's compounding interest. One should eliminate the upward battle and cruise downward instead.

In terms of investment, nobody gets rich quickly. The exceptions to the rule often don't remain rich. For example, sweepstakes winners frequently lose the money they obtained and end up where they were before. The way one behaves financially determines one's wealth. One is not talking about historical income and inherited wealth but what one can do now in terms of personal financial no matter what degree of wealth one has. Sather (2021) continues that if one's spending prevents one form taking advantage of interest, one will fight that battle all one's life. Sather encourages people to show disregard for the future and to live with an attitude of abundance and self-sufficiency rather than one of insufficiency. If one takes to heart his advice, he says one is better than 90% of the world.

Investing in the Financial Markets: Limit Risk with Knowledge

When one thinks of stewardship, one tends to think of giving; stewardship has many meanings but is generally seen as the ability to oversee or take care one's belongings. I believe we, as people, are all here for a reason, and as was discussed in the introduction with the general systems theory and interactive social system, we do not operate appropriately alone, but together. Yes, the world is not perfect, and this is one of the reasons that the wealth and income gap persists. I also believe we must understand that what we have is given by God. Therefore, as stewards, we need to learn to manage what we have since we are trusted to do so, and that includes managing ourselves so that we can help others. I have found that when I give truly and appropriately with a sound heart, I receive more blessings.

Many investors are well-off because of their net return on investment rather than the time span of their investment. One must consider various attitudes when looking to invest. As an educator in terms of the "small picture and big picture" economically, I like to envision investing in a micro and macroeconomic sense in which one has a mindset to investigate investments from different perspectives. From a macro standpoint, an investor can look at the nation or industry and decide which geographical area to invest in and if the "positives" of investing there are good to go! Another method is to choose a certain company first, or one can combine both tactics with a worldwide manager who takes care of one's business, so long as the manager has the experience and expertise in studying and analyzing the market to foresee potential gains.

Major Asset Groups

Cash, stocks, and bonds are the best-known asset groups and are mainly picked for investment in terms of retirement and postsecondary education savings strategies. These major investments are not alone in the minds of investors as additional investments such as commodities and real estate are also considered even though they usually have risks. Therefore, no matter which of the investments one chooses, one needs to do the research and ensure one is making the right choice. Stocks are of the best investments along with bonds and cash. Investment in stocks involves risks, but the trade-off can be high yields.

Bonds are not as risky and provide a more moderate yield, and some classes of bonds present great returns parallel to those of stocks. But these bonds are recognized as risky and like stocks bring greater risk. Cash and cash equivalents like treasury bills, savings deposits, and money market accounts are considered safe but have the smallest returns of the top three asset groups. The main worry about this type of investment is the risk of inflation that can outperform and eat into positive yields in time (U.S. Securities and Exchange Commission, n.d.).

To comprehend what stocks are, one must understand the market in general. The New York Stock Exchange and Nasdaq will be discussed thoroughly in Chapter 6. Understanding the market involves, as I like to tell my business pupils, sound economics that involve the effects of supply and demand, causes and outcomes of various situations, and yes, Uncle Sam's activities as well! Dorson (2020) says that putting stock securities under the microscope to decipher which ones are best can be unnerving. Many experienced investors already know ahead of time which securities to choose in reference to their planned portfolio due to specific helpful numbers that statistically aid in their choice and not just mere guesstimating or pointers provided. One can benefit in various ways from assessing and examining the volatility versus the compensation of stocks. It is important to seek stocks that are a good deal and have probable growth.

Warren Buffett explains how to make use of stocks, and it varies according to one's plans and outlook. He delivered a listing of 20 stocks with the biggest market capitalization that involved top companies. He then asked his audience which of the stocks they thought would stay in the next three decades. Buffett then talked about the top corporations in terms of market capitalization in the year 1989 and emphasized that none of them are still in the top 20 today. Buffet says that back in the day, one was certain just like Wall Street was, as one is today, but global conditions in terms of investments and other facets can alter tremendously. Buffett used the example of automobile corporations in the early 1900s, stating that around 2,000 corporations started because of the apparently incredible future. Yet in 2009, only three remained and two had to be bailed out (Locke, 2021; Pound, 2021).

Investment assets such as stocks (which differ), bonds (risk is contingent on the varying types), and funds can all be beneficial to those who want to invest, but one must have knowledge and do the proper research before choosing. Stocks entail owning a share (being a shareholder) of a specific company and can provide good returns if sound research is done. There are various funds to invest in like sector funds which involve investing in a certain industry, income funds which have stock that pays steady dividends, growth funds that may not pay regular dividends but have potential for big monetary profits, and index funds that track a certain market (Chen, 2021a). Exchange Traded Funds (ETFs) are amassed stocks that are traded like stocks with prices going up and down daily. ETFs will be discussed further in Chapter 6. Mutual funds are gathered stocks which are active (recurrent buying and selling with more risk and larger fees) while index funds are passively managed (copy a certain benchmark). These securities and investments will also be further discussed in Chapter 6.

Green (2021) explains investors will have better success if they keep in mind that controlling their feelings is important. They must not be too confident when profits are big or nervous when investments are unsuccessful. In addition, one should understand investing before participating in investment because insufficient knowledge can be worse than going by one's feelings. Moreover, diversification is imperative because mishaps will happen and one needs mental fortitude. Finally, he says that the best way to succeed in investing is to research the assets that have been performing most bleakly over the past few years and then work out whether those misfortunes are brief or long-lasting.

Tony DiPietro has worked in the world of education for over 25 years, and he provides a brief introduction to help one understand the world of saving and investing. He is a registered representative and investment advisor representative of Voya Financial Advisors.

Some terms one may have heard of when discussing investing are stocks, bonds, and mutual funds. Tony explains:

> A stock, common stock, represents a share ownership or equity in a business. For the sake of discussion, we will talk about ownership in a publicly traded company. Investors who own stock are also known as shareholders for they own a share or part of the business. Companies issue and sell shares of their business to generate capital for operations and expansion. Investors purchase shares of stock with the anticipation of these shares appreciating in value as the business grows. For example, ABC company needs $200,000 for expansion of their business; they may issue 10,000 shares at a price of $20 per share. An investor can purchase as many shares as they may like (up to the number of shares available) to take part in the ownership and growth of that company. In this case, let's say John purchases 100 shares at $20 a share for at total price of $20,000. John provides the business with $20,000 of capital investment, and in return, he now owns a percentage of the business and would participate in the growth of the business through his ownership of shares. As the business grows and the share price increases, so will his investment. A year later, the share price rises $5 a share, and now each share is worth $25. John's investment is now worth $25,000 ($20,000 initial purchase plus $5000 increase in value).

On the other hand, bonds are debt instruments; we commonly would refer to them as loans. When an entity (government, school, business, etc.) needs money for expansion, improvements, or special projects, they will seek those funds through a bond issue. An entity determines how much money is needed and then issues a number of bonds for a specific amount, maturity date, and interest rate. For example, if XYC municipality needed to finance a fire truck that cost $500,000, they may issue 500 bonds with a price of $1000 each with a 10-year maturity date and an interest rate of 1%. If an investor purchases 10 bonds for a total of $10,000, they in return would receive $100 a year in interest and at maturity, after 10 years, receive their principal of $10,000. Over the period of 10 years, the investor receives $1000 in interest and return of the principal of $10,000 for a total of $11,000.

Every investment involves some element of risk. Hence, diversification of one's investments through asset allocation helps reduce some of the risk of loss of one's principal or initial investment. One may choose a combination of stocks and bonds to build a portfolio which meets one's overall investment objectives through investing in mutual funds. Mutual funds provide investors with further diversification, asset allocation, and professional management through an active approach utilizing a fund manager to manage the fund portfolio. A passive approach might be used through investing in index funds in which the portfolio of that fund would follow an index, such as the Standard & Poors 500 or the Dow Jones Industrial Index, to name two. There are currently thousands of mutual funds available to help investors attain their investment goals and objectives. It is wise to talk with an investment professional to assist in selecting a fund that fits your needs and helps you reach your investment goals.

We would all like to earn a little bit more for the hours and effort we put into our 9 to 5 job. The best way to earn more in your current job is to love what you do. I would always tell my students to follow their passion and make it a career. If you do this, you will never work a day in your life. Your earning potential will grow as you continue to follow your passion. The psychological fulfillment of doing what you love will have an exponential impact on your quality of life. Following your passion along with a strong work ethic and positive attitude will continue to be your best friend and increase your ability to earn more from your career or job. I know this sounds like a cliché; however, no matter your income, if you do not save any of it through saving or general investing, it really doesn't matter how much you earn. The key to earning money is to save some of it for a rainy day and also have your savings work for you.

One thing I have learned over time is that one should never be too proud to work. The best leaders take pride in their work and the work of their teammates. They also would say there is never a job that is beneath them. You should never be too proud to do a task which you would ask others to do. This builds morale and sets an example for your team or family of coworkers. Being a team player will display your positive attitude and will open doors for advancement, hence increasing your earning potential.

Along with a positive attitude, thinking outside the box, networking, and listening to others will help you find new ideas and means to earn more. Another great saying is "Where there is a will, there is a way." Sometimes, life will throw you curve balls, or you may be off track for a time. Your ability to remain positive and build relationships with others will help get you through those tough times.

Now, that I just provided ways to help build your personal work value, let's get into increasing your physical/monetary earning potential by identifying ways to make more money. There are many ways to earn more money, for example, improving one's education, working more hours by taking on a part-time or seasonal job, or starting a small business (a "side hustle").

Furthering one's education can lead to advancements in one's career and also open up doors for other opportunities. The more we learn, the more we can help others and help ourselves become more valuable from an earning perspective. The more you learn about your skills and how to improve them, the more value you add. Education, whether formal or informal, is the key to our growth and will lead to further advancements and opportunities as we develop in our careers.

For example, I used to work as an administrator at a college. As I continued my education to earn my master's degree, I not only increased my salary, but it opened doors for me to teach courses at night. My earning potential went up significantly because I offered more to my position by earning a higher degree, and the high-level degree also provided me with the opportunity to instruct college level classes. When enrollment declined in the summer months, I would teach surfing lessons to make a few extra dollars. I found a way to create a "side hustle" and follow my passions of teaching, surfing, and being at the beach to earn more money.

CHAPTER 5

WHERE THE MONEY COMES FROM AND HOW TO GET FINANCIAL SECURITY

People, Businesses, Factors of Production, and Money Flow

Microeconomics is the portion of economics which involves the decisions and interaction of individual consumers, households, government, and businesses. Microeconomics involves measuring the of price of products, the actual employees within the business, and the income of the business and households as well as expenditures (amount of money spent) of the government, households, and businesses. Economic stakeholders are apprehensive about such facets as what products one should buy, which products should be made and at what price, as well as if and when the government should intervene. In addition, economics indulges in what are hopefully efficient and effective markets that encourage competition. Market structures ranging from high to low barrier entry (monopoly, oligopoly, monopolistic competition, pure "perfect" competition) explain what markets are good or not so good for society. The basic supply and demand aspects are the general focus in the market economy (see market economy in the coming sections), and the use of the circular flow chart demonstrates this circular repetitious movement by households and businesses.

I always like to explain to my business students that business, economics, and marketing are all interrelated, with business being the center piece containing the others. Unless a student is pursuing a specific narrowed down major in one of these subjects, therefore, when asked the question which major is best, I say business because each of these aspects will be taught in one shape or form within the business curriculum. In terms of interrelationship, the same can hold true about spending, expenses, saving, and investment. These facets are all intertwined as one can affect the other, both positively and negatively, involving one's income, expenses, and saving and investment potential.

Income and Expenses, Saving and Investments

Alfred Edmond Jr., Senior Vice President and Editor-at-large of Black Enterprise wrote in 2017, explaining that the capability to create wealth varies on the level we manage our spending, so that after salary and other taxes, and for needs such as housing, food, and transportation, there is still some left to save for emergencies future expenditures, retirement, investment portfolio, purchasing real estate, financing businesses, and obtaining other assets (Wright, 2020).

Income and expenses can be simply explained as the money that is taken in and is spent. The unadorned truth for frugality is to spend less so that one has no budget shortfall which can only be fixed by borrowing funds, spending less, or acquiring more income. Therefore, it is imperative to make good personal spending choices (opportunity cost), plan, and budget. One does not have to live a boring life but trading off some comfort and waste of money now (eating out frequently, expensive material goods) for some positive "autonomy" (retirement, education, property) later may make all the difference in the world.

In addition, one may have to spend money that one may not want to due to savings. Such aspects as taking care of one's needs to stay healthy and home repairs along with the first three levels of Maslow's hierarchy need to be tended to early and when needed. If these matters are not attended to, they can add up, causing an abundance of problems and making one worse off. Perhaps one can partake in the 50-20-30 rule in which 50% of one's income will go to necessities such as bills, 20% to paying debt and savings, and 30% for self wants (Levels 4 and 5 of Maslow's hierarchy). Another rule one could adopt is the 70-20-10 mindset in which 70% earned is consumed, 20% is saved, and 10% bestowed to others. No matter what approach one may utilize, income and expenses have a profound impact on one's choice to save and or invest.

To save or invest? That is the question! Although saving and investing are the same to many, the two can be poles apart in that saving can simply be to provide financial security, money put away just in case it is needed while investing is done to acquire wealth, to grow one's money, or obtain a return on investment in stocks, bonds, or property. A big difference between the two is in liquidity. Liquidity is equity or the ability for an asset to be changed into cash. Saving is considered more liquid because the cash is at hand, while investing is not as liquid due to the risks involved as well as the time value of money.

Time is imperative in terms of the value of money. In times when prearranged investments are greater than strategic savings, one's income is greater. Therefore, more income means more savings which means savings are equivalent to envisioned investment. The antithesis is that in times when savings are larger than prearranged investments, the level of income goes down. The bottom line is to invest and save so one can prepare for the future and produce income by creating a savings account and investing knowledgably to acquire a high return on investment with a diversified portfolio.

Budget Line

The economic problems of the individual expand into society. As for the individual, the problem lies with the income factor. Our wants are greater than the means to get what we want. If we do have enough income, the choice factor comes into effect in terms of which products we choose and which we forgo. A budget line is a sound microeconomic graph that displays a combination of two products a buyer can purchase with a certain set income.

"How Choices Today Influence Your Lifestyle Tomorrow"

Rosalind S. Robinson, Doctor of Theology, freelance writer and editor quotes Jeremiah 29:11 (NIV): "For I know the plans I have for you, declares the Lord, plans to *prosper you* and not to harm you, plans to give you hope and a future." She reflects:

> We're a product of heredity, environment, and traditions. We were born into and taught certain things. At some point in our lives, we decide

to continue those same traditions or to go in a different direction. For example, a child from a good home might go astray. Peer pressure, curiosity, or maybe even defiance might be a factor. On the other hand, a child born into poverty or abuse may decide to live a better life. They decide not to repeat the cycle. It's all about choices. It's also how we distinguish good and bad as sometimes everything may look good from the outside, but we never really know exactly what's going on inside. As human beings, we sometimes make very good choices, and other times, we regret some of the decisions we make.

I grew up with both parents in the household. Whether we were rich or poor wasn't a concern of mine as a child. I just knew that I was being provided for and I was happy. Later in life, I realized we were neither rich nor poor but lived a "rich" life because we had what we needed, and we were happy for the most part.

I remember being in grammar school and having a savings account with Howard Savings Bank. I would take my bank book to school along with my money and give it to my teacher. At some point, I would get my bank book back showing my balance and interest. It's funny now because I recall my teacher explaining interest and being intrigued by that concept of getting something extra. I remember writing about that experience in a journal entry; however, being so young, I had heard the word interest but wasn't sure if it was 'entrance' or 'interest.' I can clearly remember writing it both ways and crossing it out numerous times because I just didn't know. I'm not sure what was going on that day, but I didn't have an opportunity to look it up at school. For some reason, it stuck with me all day. When I got home that evening, I looked it up to make sure I would know how to write it next time.

How is this relevant to the topic? It was something I was exposed to at an early age. My mother and my teacher were both proactive in teaching me values that would have an impact on my future. I chose to grasp that information.

When I was about 12, I would go to Bingo with my friend and her mother. The owner of the snack stand saw us there so often that he offered us a job (without pay), but we could collect tips. My first thought? I could put the money in my account and gain more interest. It just became a goal. Throughout the years, I continued doing odd jobs such as babysitting and braiding hair. Upon graduating from high school, I found a summer job, my first full-time job. Upon receiving my very first check, I opened another account with Howard Savings Bank. Every pay day, I would walk to the bank (several blocks away) excited to deposit my check.

What am I saying? Did my environment set me on this track? I would say yes. Perhaps I would have learned to save on my own at some point. Perhaps I could have had this experience and thought nothing of it or done nothing about it. It's all about choices. Even if you're not exposed to managing finances, some things you ultimately learn and apply for yourself. Yes, we all experience hardship, but you must always have a plan. That plan may require spending less on those things you enjoy. It's called sacrifice. You can't continue doing the same thing and expect different results.

When I was an educator at an urban high school, my students would often ask my opinion about things. They trusted me. On one occasion, a student had a desire to work full time and not pursue higher education. It's always a good idea to just listen and allow young adults to figure things out themselves. When asked what the plan was, he pretty much had things mapped out. I commended him for that, but then the conversation went a little deeper. The budget he had in mind was for a teenager living at home with his mom, with limited responsibilities, so it seemed ideal. I decided to present another scenario, one using the same income but this time with more responsibilities like rent, utilities, food, possibly a car, repairs, gas; well, you get the idea. If you've noticed, there's no mention of eating out, movies, shopping, and other extra things. Without criticizing or condemning this young man, I just opened his eyes to facts. You might ask why a Language Arts Teacher would have this kind of conversation with her students. You might even say it's the responsibility of their parents. Well, if it takes a village, then we must assume the responsibility of sharing what we know and those things that will impact future generations. For me, it was wanting the very same things for my students that I wanted for my own son. In essence I emphasized the importance of maintaining good credit, paying bills on time, living within one's means, saving and/or investing, preparing for the future, and creating generational wealth.

Let's refer Jeremiah 29:11. The Bible promises that God has a plan for our lives. That promise includes but is not limited to our finances. Anything is possible if we believe; however, we have a role to play in the process. Learn to combine your purpose with your passion. I love to write, edit, and teach. I have a passion for it. My purpose is helping and encouraging others. That's what makes me a successful educator, mentor, and writer.

Finally, you might ask how having a savings account as a child molded me as an adult. Well, let's just say that the experience followed me all the days of my life. I still value saving, sharing, and investing. I continue to believe in paying debt on time, minimizing credit card use, and yes, I get excited about having a high credit score.

Lastly, let's not make it any one person's responsibility to teach our kids about money and finances. Just as I got my first lesson in grammar school, I believe we should start them off at a very early age. Parents, teachers, online classes, workshops, whatever it takes. What we teach them today will possibly impact their future.

Dr. Robison lays out a great example of how to be frugal with her own experiences, demonstrating her thorough background of budgeting and saving for the right reasons so that she can help support herself and family as well as bless others. Such positive actions and good living aid in one's present and future endeavors and can also involve one's retirement arrangements.

MONEY HAS NO COMPLEXION

Automated Savings and Retirement Plans

Without the proper discipline and know-how that Dr. Robinson exhibited, saving money can be easier said than done. Whether one saves money in a jar or makes use of automated savings accounts, the idea of putting aside money is beneficial. Automated savings allows for the deposit of money from a current account. The key to these accounts is to make sure one understands the monthly fees that are charged. One can begin this account by transferring a small mount and add more cash each month on the same day.

Establishing a sound plan and budget is crucial to the overall financial well-being of a person, and alternative ways to acquire additional income can range from employment opportunities to sources of income like automated savings and investing. If one is fortunate enough to have a job, whether one is self-employed or tied to a firm, additional employment opportunities may be available, and to what degree depends on the place of work. Sometimes, a retirement plan is in place and, in some instances, may be mandatory for the good of the employee.

Cheng (2021) explained that plans like a conventional individual retirement accounts (IRA) and 401(k) and 403(b) plans and annuities are also valuable in terms of retirement savings that can be beneficial to future endeavors. The conventional IRA is for those employees who would rather set aside money on their own or increase their retirement reserves. This conventional account can be obtained by those who are working (and taxed) even if the job does not have a plan and in most cases can be written off on one's taxes. The great news is that one can capitalize in terms of investing in several assets such as exchange traded funds and mutual funds.

This IRA is ideal when companies do not have a 401(k) or 403(b) plan which can also aid in building wealth. A 401(k) is a prearranged employer supported provision pension account that takes money out of the employee's pay and, in many cases, can be matched by the company. A 403(b) is the same as the 401(k) which is sponsored by private for-profit entities, except that the 403(b) is sponsored by government or nonprofit entities. Tax-extractions in terms of retirement (Roth IRA) are also good for those people who want to indulge in that type of retirement fund. This type of retirement benefit has a two-pronged advantage in that one is not taxed when one gets their money after retirement. Also, one can take money out of the account before retirement if need be and will not be penalized.

For those married couples who are not fully employed (one is unemployed), the ability to acquire spousal IRA may also be an option offered by the employer, and it operates just like a regular IRA with a couple minor adjustments. This account allows an employed spouse to make a payment to an IRA in the name of an unemployed spouse just if they are married and filled jointly. In addition, those who consider enhancing their retirement reserve plans can also get involved with annuities with the sequence of disbursements made at equivalent periods, such as variable, indexed, and fixed pensions.

Variable annuities (what I like to call the "home run annuity" because one is looking for the big gain) is a type of investment one may seek because it offers large returns, but there is a trade-off! RISK! This is due to the focus on the performance of the portfolios of various accounts chosen. Indexed annuities, although more cautious than variable annuities, still have risks in terms of disbursing an interest rate centered on the success of certain market indexes like the Dow Jones, Nasdaq, and S&P 500. If the market is fruitful, then Bang! "Home run!" If not, it can be a "swing and a miss and potential loss!"

Fixed annuities, in my view, are the best of the annuities for the simple fact that a set interest rate is applied no matter what happens in the market. This is good for the beginner investor and those who want peace of mind. These annuities are based on the assured interest rate, and income is not affected by market instability as one knows precisely how much income will be paid.

In terms of insurance-based investments, one's primary concern should be the economic stability and performance of the entity one is investing in. Other important considerations depend on whether one is looking for a whole life product, a universal life product, or an annuity (Dorson, 2020). One must consider that no matter what one's profession is (military, sport, entertainment, business, academia, blue- or white-collar employment), certain retirement benefits are available through the job or local, state, and federal entities. Professional development advisors, counselors, coaches, and financial planners can also provide valuable information regarding these matters.

When choosing an advisor, one should research several before making a choice. It is inadvisable to try to find an advisor on one's own, and one must comprehend how the consultant is compensated. One should employ a financial consultant one can trust who has a client-centered focus with the right expertise and qualifications. In addition, one should ensure the consultant is in line with one's financial plan (Smart Asset, 2021). In doing so, one can have amazing potential and knowledge in investing especially in the stock market involving the Dow Jones, Nasdaq, and the S&P 500.

CHAPTER 6

PUT YOUR PAPER ON THE BIG BOARD: PROFITING FROM THE STOCK MARKET AND INVESTMENT ACCOUNTS

The Big Dogs: Nasdaq, Dow Jones, and S&P 500

One cannot understand investing without understanding the Big Board and how market indexes operate. The New York Stock Exchange which uses the Dow Jones Industrial Average (DJIA index) is a larger exchange since its market capitalization is greater, but the National Association of Securities Dealers Automated Quotations (Nasdaq) has a larger trading volume. The Nasdaq composite helps investors to sell and purchase stocks on a robotic technological translucent processer (Nasdaq) that measures the alteration in over 3,000 stocks exchanged on the Nasdaq Exchange.

While the DJIA measures the fluctuations of 30 large domestic United States corporations, the Nasdaq composite tracks both domestic U.S. companies and foreign entities. The S&P 500 (benchmark index) is merely an index that follows 500 big corporations itemized on the United States stock exchanges and is an investment instrument that helps decipher the condition of the general economy. The only downfall with this measurement is that it leaves out the mid to smaller capitalizations stocks in the nation, emphasizing just the "big dogs" or large capitalization stocks which compose most of the index (Pant, 2021).

Stock Investment: Mutual, Index, and Exchange Traded Funds

Many people think investments are the same in terms of funds, but such is not the case. Index funds and mutual funds are acquired for various reasons with different actions. Mutual funds invest in an altering inventory of securities preferred by an investing manager while index funds involve the concentration of a certain inventory of securities of listed corporations alone (S&P 500, Dow Jones, Nasdaq). Index funds are a perfect way to invest because one is making the decisions on one's own in terms of creating a well-planned portfolio in which the behavior or percentage of segments of the market is being observed. Investing in index funds is more ideal for long-term investment, and one who is a beginner should be wary of this type of investment.

"Compared with managed funds, index funds offer better average returns, in large part because their expenses are lower" (Glassman, 2021, p. 31). Compared to stocks, index funds are for those individuals who do not prefer to put all their marbles into one bag but like to diversify making use of an assorted (basket) portfolio so that their investments can "balance out" in case one or some investments go under. More experienced and confident investors may choose to invest in a single entity after having past success or because they have profound knowledge of the chosen company.

When one purchases shares within an entity, one becomes a proportional proprietor of the entity. This means that one receives a portion of the earnings or deficits depending on how well the entity performs. Stakeholders who have purchased proprietorship in profitable entities have become wealthy. Occasionally, companies fail. This can happen gradually or wind up in a disastrous failure. If one has stock in these entities, then one's stake may be valueless.

When one partakes in an index fund, one is purchasing a diversified basket of stocks intended to follow a certain index such as the Dow Jones Industrial Average or the S&P 500. Therefore, purchasing stake in an index fund means one possesses shares of stock in many companies. Statistically, 50% of stocks *have* to be below average, and 50% of stocks *have* to be above average. This is why countless investors are so enthusiastic about passive index fund investing. One does not have to devote countless hours annually to viewing one's portfolio.

One who invests in stocks in a specific company has to have sound knowledge and do research to become cognizant of the company's financial health and business strategies. One should decide with one's certified financial advisor which method is most suited to one's circumstances. Overall, index fund investing is preferable to investing in individual stocks because it incurs minimum expenses, eliminates the need to continuously analyze company documents and performance, and ensure one is "average" which is much better than losing one's money in a bad investment (Kennon, 2021).

When one looks at mutual funds, this type of investment can be easily explained in lay terms. As a college professor, I tell my students that writing can be depicted as a bowl of soup. The bowl of soup smells and tastes good, but when you look in it, one cannot really see what makes the soup smell and taste so good. Therefore, I tell students who need help in making their writing clear to take heed of the soup analogy which is as follows: In order to get a better perspective of what is in the soup, before putting the ingredients in the boiling water, one can separate them on a plate to see what the ingredients are. One can put the seasoning, carrots, meat, potatoes, onion, and any other ingredients separately on the plate so one can see what the bowl of soup is composed of. The same holds true for mutual funds. The mutual funds are like a pot of soup composed of various ingredients (stocks and bonds), and when one purchases a share, one is getting a scoop of the pot of soup.

Investment in mutual funds (actively managed) is less predictable and has higher charges. Investment in index funds is a good method to grow one's gains into lifetime financial well-being (Friedberg 2021c). These investments which are composed of stocks that reflect the corporation and execution of a market index, such as the S&P 500, Nasdaq, and Dow Jones, are a differentiated and affordable method to capitalize in the stock market and are also managed passively with lesser charges than funds that are actively managed and with a greater return on investment. The good news with mutual funds is that they provide routine investments and the ability to take money out at any time. These funds operate by extracting money from investors, and a fund manager invests it in stocks and bonds and other financial tools, following a market index, which requires less research and is less expensive. Investing in this manner is simple, safe, and easy to do. First, one selects the index that one wants to follow; second, one picks a fund that follows one's chosen index; and finally, one purchases shares in the index fund. One may ponder what the advantage is in seeking mutual funds. The general answer is that one can have a manager do investing, according to one's needs, which provides one with an affordable way to invest.

Warren Buffett explains that index funds are the way and that one should be diverse in one's investments over time. This is his motive for making the trustee responsible for his estate put 90% of his money into the S&P 500 and 10% in treasury bills for his spouse when he passes away. In a nutshell, the greatest aspect in terms of investing is to purchase 90% in the S&P 500 index fund (Locke, 2021). So, the main differences between a mutual fund and an index fund is the way that the two are managed (actively or passively), the manner in which the stock performs, and the actual costs that one is charged. Exchange Traded Funds (ETFs) can also be used as index funding as they can be bought and sold like stock as well.

Assessment of Mutual Funds

The listed items from a mutual fund provide much information and should be viewed before partaking in the investment. Mutual funds are composed of various investments; therefore, one should research the goals of the investment funds as well as the costs and risks. Deciphering the manner in which a fund acquired its yields is as important as examining the yields so that one can compare the fund with other funds to see if it meets one's goals in terms of one's portfolio. Furthermore, assessing mutual funds involves determining how the funds are managed, looking at the type of investments they have (whether one or many), what the fund concentrates on, the historical performance, risks, and volatility, and other costs (Dorson, 2020). Overall, mutual funds help to diversify one's portfolio, but exchange traded funds are even better, if understood.

Exchange Traded Funds (ETFs)

ETFs are an assemblage of stocks, bonds, real estate, and commodities which all can be obtained in a diverse manner that trade like a stock and are bought and sold with shifting prices daily. This type of investment provides one with essentially minor minimums and control, but one can only purchase and sell shares in market transactions. In addition, investment funds and ETFs can be inexpensive ways to win in the market, but like everything else about investment, there can be risks.

ETFs, have received much attention recently. At first, one may perceive ETFs as being identical to mutual funds because they comprise a myriad of investments, and the earnings are centered on how that mixture performs. Nonetheless, there are differences. Most important, ETFs are simple to buy and sell, while many mutual fund investments need one to hold them for a period of time or incur extra costs (Ask Money, 2020). Research is imperative so that one comprehends what the investments are and is confident in one's strategy. In this way, one can recognize the differences of the index fund so that one can select a cost-effective investment that suits one's needs.

Mutual, Index, and Exchange Traded Funds: Positives and Negatives

Mutual funds are one of the leading choices of investing in the United States. Benefits for investors are "advanced portfolio managing, dividend reinvestment, risk reduction, convenience, and fair pricing." The drawbacks are "high fees, tax inefficiency, poor trade performance, and potential for management abuses" (Palmer, 2021, p.1).

The benefits of index funds are that they provide a simple way to trace the general well-being of a market. By observing a single numerical amount, it is simple to estimate the present state of the market. Also, the past statistics of index funds and prices can give some direction to investors in terms of how the markets have performed in the past, which helps in the decision-making process.

The chief benefit is that because they simply trace stock indexes, they are passively managed, which means low fees. Exchange traded funds are often index funds, and they usually offer the lowest fees of all. In addition, index funds permit investors to attain their objectives in reference to targets more reliably.

Shortcomings are that there are problems with the computation of stock indexes that can turn into disadvantages. Higher-priced stocks have a bigger influence on movements in the index than lower-priced stocks. The index is price-weighted, so no thought is given to the relative size of the industry sector of the stock or its market capitalization. Another criticism of the Dow Jones Industrial Average is that it signifies a small part of the investment world because it contains only 30 firms.

Furthermore, the lack of flexibility confines index funds to well-established investment approaches and sectors, they cannot to copy the most thriving fund managers' methods, and managers are continually developing innovative approaches. Even the most successful approaches will not produce good imitations of exchange traded funds in the near future (Edwards, 2020).

An advantage of ETFs over mutual funds is that they have some very attractive aspects such as tax benefits whereas when one sells a stake in mutual funds, one can have a tax obligation. ETFs are swapped on an exchange instead of being purchased and sold by a fund proprietor; therefore, a tax charge is not generated when one sells. In addition, the price of ETF shares is less than mutual funds, including passive index as well. An important asset of an ETF is that it has greater liquidity than a mutual fund. If one purchases into a mutual fund, in many cases, one has to hold that share for a length of time before one can sell it without weakening the fund or paying extra fees.

Other disadvantages are that ETFs that trace a stock index are soundly diverse while others are not. Since so many are assiduously fixated, they can trigger synthetic inflation in the markets, if they do well for a period time. To conclude, actively managed ETFs could use tactics that are unverified in time, which indicates an alteration in market circumstances which can initiate a meaningful cost in worth (Ask Money, 2020). Mutual, index, and exchange traded funds are all great investments, and with proper knowledge of one's own or the use of a robo-advisor, the investments are an even greater choice.

Robo-Advisors

Robo-advisors provide another way to get help and valuable information in terms of investing. These valuable alphanumeric investment managers tend to one's exclusive monetary needs and perform calculations in reference to automated reasoning as the technology gathers one's thinking and does the investing for one.

Robo-advisors are comparable to conventional financial information except the robo-advisor executes a sequence of computations in terms of one's monetary plans, risk tolerance, and position in the market. These computations are an advantage in that they can be done faster than by a real person and eliminate the emotional influence in making choices. The choices created are based on one's portfolio provisions and can be occasionally adjusted to ensure that one's savings are maintained to one's investment objectives.

"This brings us to an important investment concept. No matter what investment objective you may have, or what your intended holding period is, or what kind of stock analysis is performed: If you do not have a diversified portfolio, you are either throwing away return or assuming risk that could be avoided, or both.... Your investment strategy should deal with the overall, long-term guidelines you set to meet your financial goals" (Littauer, 1994, p.1). Long term investment will be discussed further in chapter 11 with a sound example from 'Big Al,' college administrator, and frugal lifestyle and simple investor.

The first question to ask oneself is whether one really needs a robo-advisor and if so what type. There are various electronic advisors available, but they are all tailored to provide specific help to individuals. Therefore, it is important for one to make sure getting this help is of personal value and to know how it operates. Once this is taken into consideration, researching and selecting the right advisor about charges, smallest amounts invested, and amenities is essential. Robo-advisors are plentiful and come in a broad spectrum from general to tailor-cut, giving anyone a chance to obtain a robo-advisor that suits their precise desires and financial situation, from a long-time investor with experience to a beginner seeking to commence a retirement account with reserves from their employment.

One can decide which advisor to pick by determining one's needs and wants. Now, those who are experienced and have large portfolios may want to deal with real people in terms of planning. Finally, one should specifically review whether robo-advisors have low fees, are free of charge, have real people consultants, display specifics with graphs, and have apps and software (Friedberg, 2021e). In general, one can distribute the cash in one's portfolio into numerous funds or ETFs (see previous section), based on one's age and risk tolerance. One can also achieve more multifaceted portfolio repairs as needed, for less cost (Roberge, 2019). Some more pluses and minuses are further discussed in the next sections.

Robo-Advisor Plusses and Nixes

Robo-advisors have low costs whereas an actual person advising usually costs 1% to 2% of one's portfolio's worth annually. Robo-advisors cost a portion of that, regularly 0.25% to 0.5% of one's portfolio worth, and they do not regularly make one pay commissions to purchase or sell assets in one's account or to reconfigure one's portfolio. These automated advisors also reconfigure one's portfolio so that one does not flow external to one's goal in terms of asset allocation, meeting one's portfolio necessities and goals. The asset allocation can be altered as time goes by according to one's age and various other factors.

Robo-advisors make use of diversification in order to reduce risk by scattering one's investments transversely to businesses, market capitalizations, and other assets with the use of exchange traded funds. These ETFs transform multiple stocks and in many cases are just index funds that reflect a chief stock market index such as the S&P 500 or Nasdaq (see previous chapter)

Easy access and affordability are another positive for robo-advisors. A real person as an advisor mainly takes people with a greater financial value. This value differs but starts at a high minimum because these consultants make their money based on the scope of the portfolios they manage. Some robo-advisors may even demand the smallest investment; many do not and let everybody, no matter their financial status, invest with no particular comprehension or prior prosperity.

Many investments do not do well for the simple reason that people intertwine their emotions in their decision-making process by responding to the market and its current performance instead of viewing the extended prospects. In addition, as stocks drop, investors get thrown into mental disarray and sell. This action generates a malicious sequence of purchasing above what is usual and selling low, permitting amateurish investors to exhaust their money on stocks instead of earning it. Therefore, the robo-advisor is a good investor. This technology invests based on thorough, extended term investing instead of fearful or eager premonitions (Davis, 2021). Robo-advisors are not expensive and, in many cases, do not require the minimum balance. They also tend to stick to optimized indexed plans that are tailored for most investors. One must understand that robo-advisers are not human beings which limits one's personal contact and viewpoint in terms of flexibility and personalization. Therefore, one's sentiments cannot be catered to due to lack of human interface. Robo-advisors do not propose lots of choices for investor flexibility, are inclined to toss muck in the face of conventional advice-giving services, and do not provide person-to-person collaboration (Friedberg, 2021b).

Furthermore, an automated system can create advice founded only on the data delivered to the technology. This data is typically confined to essential aspects that can be enumerated such as one's age, one's outlook, and how comfortable one is in terms of risk-taking. One's motives (*why* one is investing) are only as important to creating the correct investment choices as age and risk tolerance. An automated system cannot assess these facets, and the technology cannot offer one counsel in reference to challenging, sensitive, or personal situations (Roberge, 2019).

The ideal investor to seek a robo-advisor would be one who is new or has little experience in investing. As was discussed earlier in previous chapters in terms of investing securities and other assets, many people do not have time or the desire to do the research to learn about these investment aspects. Therefore, they give this task to the robo-advisor. A major factor is one's financial situation. This electronic technology does the work for the not-so-wealthy to gain admittance to the sort of proficiency that was not accessible to them years ago. Just as long these investors understand the simple basics of technology, they will be comfortable with using these automatic advisors. With no anxiety, stress, or exertion, one just accumulates wealth by way of automated technology (Davis, 2021).

CHAPTER 7

BE STIRRED AND NOT SHAKEN: EMBRACE BOND INVESTING

When making any type of investment, one must understand the primary and secondary markets. The primary market involves the government, corporations, and municipal entities while the secondary market includes stock exchanges like the Nasdaq and NYSE where trading is done by investors, as discussed in the previous chapter. The primary market is difficult to gain entrée to in terms of buying individual bonds while the secondary market is less obvious or clear.

Napoletano & Curry (2021) explain that bonds involve a loan to an entity such as the government, a company, or municipality at a fixed rate of return, keeping in mind that the worth of the bond can alter in the future. Bonds enable an entity to raise money by borrowing money and reimbursing it with interest at a fixed rate called a coupon over a period of time. Put into lay terms, a bond is a credit from an investor to the government or entity who makes use of the funds to pay for certain expenses. In return, the investor gets a fixed rate of interest.

When individuals buy corporate bonds, unlike stocks, they don't own anything within the entity, but are the buying part of the entity's debt responsibility. The positives are that bonds are low risk (although entities could go broke), they create a diversified portfolio, provide sound cashflow, and secure a certain yield over time. Moreover, one can receive interest at steady foreseeable rates. One must remember that interest rates are low, that one needs to use a broker, and bonds cannot be exchanged publicly. The average extended return on government bonds (5%) is lower than the return on stocks (10%), but stocks have greater risks.

One can also sell bonds at a higher price than that for which they were acquired. Greater yield means a small credit rating and greater interest while the antithesis is that the investment grade means a larger credit rating and smaller interest. Although bonds do fluctuate, the fluctuations are not as extreme as the up and down movement of stocks, and they have more predictable returns; however, one should keep in mind the importance of having diverse investments. People may tend to lean towards bonds as they get older looking at the long term, but they should maintain a diversified portfolio.

Municipal bonds are often sought after because they offer the opportunity to get tax benefits, and this type of investment can be short-term or long-term. Everyone, including the municipalities, benefits from this type of investment because it helps with funding social ventures and public amenities.

Treasury bonds, derived by way of a broker or straight from the treasury, make up most of the treasury debt in the United States. These electronically distributed bonds supported by 'Uncle Sam' are safe but low-interest investments. A key factor in this investment is that one can take money out before the maturity date which can be beneficial due to the length of the investment and because bond prices and interest rates fluctuate.

The three types of treasury bonds differ in terms of maturity: treasury bills, treasury notes, and treasury bonds. Maturity refers to the actual time when the giver of the bond gives back the money that was borrowed. Bills are offered at a discount from their face value as investors acquire the total sum once the bill reaches maturity. Notes and bonds differ in that they are offered at face value which is the price in terms of a bid and asking price. Bid refers to the highest amount a purchaser is prepared to pay for a bond while the asking price is the lowest price proposed by the seller. Treasury bonds have fixed interest rates, and interest is paid twice a year with no risk of defaulting. One can buy bonds directly, but keep in mind that the price may not be reasonable, and this can be a negative for those who are unsure or lack knowledge.

Two of the best investments one can choose in terms of bonds, depending on one's goals, are mutual funds and ETF bonds. Mutual funds are great due to the pool of investing which creates sound diversification which can be active or passive. In addition, the maturity rate can be short or extended, they are similar to stock, one can reinvest the interest, and they have tax benefits. Investing in ETF bonds can also be done actively or passively; they have even lower fees than mutual funds. This investment can be exchanged like stock during regular daily market times and not just once a day.

Investing in bonds can be done through what was explained earlier as the secondary market, stock exchanges like Nasdaq and the NYSE in which the investments are based on the face value. A high price value means stocks trade at a premium while low prices mean stocks are exchanged at a discount. Mixing one's investments is not an easy endeavor as the economic forces of supply and demand and inflation play a critical role in one's decision making. Along with these aspects, credit ratings, which are assigned by ratings agencies to bonds and their providers based on their creditworthiness, and market interest rates also have a profound impact on price (Napoletano & Curry, 2021).

Nonetheless, maintaining a diversified portfolio is once again the key. For example, Barbara Friedberg explained that if one invests in just a single stock market mutual fund, if the market drops 20% in a severe year, one's investment returns will also drop. Therefore, she recommends including a bond mutual fund with the stock market fund, creating a more diverse and safer portfolio; even if the returns on the stock market fund drop, the bond fund's returns may rise 15% (Friedberg, 2021c). Including real estate options within a portfolio makes one's investment even sounder and more stable.

Positives and Negatives of Bonds

Bond ETFs and bond mutual funds are alike in many ways, for both include various bonds, but they have two differences which involve duration of trading and taxes. Bond ETFs are traded throughout the day while bond mutual funds can only be traded one time daily at the conclusion of the market. They provide easy access to individual investors and are less expensive than purchasing bonds directly because investing in the bond market is not like investing in the stock market in terms of quickly changing assets into cash. Therefore, one does not require a lot of money because the cost entails the price of a share and not the usual costly minimum to get in (Royal, 2021c). Also, one does not have to examine a myriad of specific bonds but can opt for the types of bonds one plans to invest in such as a short-, medium-, or long-term fund. Each fund will react differently to changes in interest rates, reducing instability and risks in a diverse investment portfolio. ETFs are less expensive than purchasing bonds directly since investing in the bond market is not similar to investing in the stock market in terms of quickly changing assets into cash.

On the downside, bond ETFs give low returns due to interest rates staying low over a period of time, particularly for short-term bonds, and this is compounded by expense ratios being quite high when managed by professionals. One must also keep in mind that one's principal is not guaranteed. If interest rates are not in one's favor, the incorrect type of bond fund could decline considerably, and you will not be refunded for the decline (Royal, 2021c).

Municipal bonds have some positive attractions in that they are free from federal, state, and local tax, and this gives one who invests in these bonds the ability to gain compound interest swiftly with less instability. In addition, municipal bonds are very liquid (easily changed to cash), and they can be exchanged on the secondary market. On the flip side, municipal bonds do have a few disadvantages as well. As was discussed in Chapter 3, opportunity costs are an ongoing aspect in terms of investing as one must make decisions about trade-offs. Another disadvantage is that municipal bond yields may not outdo inflation, and the bond may go into default. Another risk involves interest rates going down which will cause a drop in value of the bonds (Pat S., 2011).

The advantages of corporate bonds are that they are diverse, liquid, and less volatile than stocks. One can select from a large number of corporate providers and bonds. In addition, the worldwide corporate bond market is very liquid. Despite this, a disadvantage of corporate bonds is that many corporate bonds have to be bought over the counter for various reasons, including their diversity. In addition, corporate bonds can be a credit risk in terms of defaulting, something one has to consider. Finally, reduced risk means lesser earnings for investors on average (Bovaird, 2021).

Government bonds are a great asset due to tax advantages and low default risk, making them a secure investment. Many enjoy this type of bond because it helps a cause instead of a business or corporation, but on the flip side, the danger in terms of lower returns and interest rates must be taken into consideration.

Bonds Investment Evaluation

Dorson (2020) says that "evaluating a bond purchase is very different from researching an individual stock" (Bonds Section, para 22). One must think about several factors when examining the potential risks and returns associated with a particular bond as well as analyze timing and liquidity issues associated with investing in bonds generally. Some of the questions one must ask concern the "type of bond to purchase, maturity, degree of risk, interest, alteration to stock securities, discounts, premiums, and yield" (Dorson, 2020, Bonds Section, para 17).

"Instead of stocks, wealthier Black households are more likely to own assets that have a reputation for being safer, such as bonds, life insurance or real estate, said Tatjana Meschede, associate director at Brandeis University's Institute on Assets and Social Policy" (Choe, 2020, para 10). Choe, 2020 continues to posit Rogers in saying that, years coupled over, Black people are still reasonably unusual in the financial industry, which is a hard trend to stop. Whites who lived in richer communities have a more comfortable time creating business and most likely getting promoted. Comparatively, there are only a little amount of Black people operating big business entities or tendering their services as financial planners. Therefore, probable Black investors may neglect purchasing stocks perceiving as though this is not a good move. Currently, about "1,200 Black certified financial planners exist in the United States" (para 27) says Ethridge, the financial adviser in the Washington area who is also on the board of the Association of African American Financial Advisors. Throughout the nation, approximately 87,000 certified financial planners are currently in total. Nonetheless, bonds are a great investment if properly understood, just as other investments such as real estate and its various forms.

CHAPTER 8

BRICK AND MORTAR PAYOFFS: IGNITE YOUR NET WORTH THROUGH REAL ESTATE INVESTING

Why invest in real estate? One reason is that it benefits one's portfolio in terms of diversification and gives one the ability to balance out securities that are high risk. In addition, real estate creates a good flow of income, has tax benefits, and has great liquidation potential. When considering real estate as an investment, most people think of it as real property, but there is a slight difference between the two. Real estate alone involves the tangible estate and constructs around it as well as the assets within its realm while real property is real estate with the legalities of proprietorship and rights to use.

There are many approaches to real estate investing, and purchasing and selling property is just one way. One can also invest in companies that gain from real estate undertakings. The key is how and why one invests in this property. Investment in residential property entails going to see the investment for oneself. Real Estate Investment Trust (REIT) investment calls for one to ensure that the persons operating the trust have a sound and reputable background and proper knowledge (Dorson, 2020).

Real Estate Investment Trust (REIT)

The 1960s were a turbulent time in the United States, and among with the various laws passed, one of the positives was the1960s income making real estate legislation that was implemented for all United States citizens. Although such legislation existed back in the previous decades, the law did not help small investors, mainly people of color, for various whys and wherefores that were discussed in the first two chapters. Since then, REITs have become popular not just with people of color but with everyone who has access, knowledge, and the ability to take advantage of real estate investment.

On September 14, 1960, President Eisenhower authorized a law that provided a fresh way to income-producing real estate investment which involved the intertwining of the preeminent qualities of real estate and stock-based investment. This act gave to all United States citizens access to the profits of real estate investment that beforehand were offered only to big business and to affluent people. The basis for the contemporary REIT age ensued with the Tax Reform Act of 1986, when REITs were afforded the capability to trade in real estate, instead of merely possessing or funding it (Nareit, 2021).

Regulated by the Internal Revenue Service, a real estate investment trust (REIT) is a liquid asset that can be exchanged on the main stock exchange, an investment in which an entity links with numerous investments to buy real estate. This action also performs like a mutual fund and permits both prominent and lesser investors to possess a portion of real estate. REITs allow for the proprietorship or funding of property like a stakeholder in a corporation having stock, except one does not have to buy it. There are two ways in which REITs can be utilized: equity and mortgage rates.

The equity route involves earning revenue from owning or renting such property as malls, apartments, hotels, and offices while the mortgage way is the gaining of revenue from interest warranted on investing (owning and buying from lenders) in mortgages and securities from both commercial and residential property. The great news is that 75% of revenue has to be derived from the entity's real estate rent and interest sales from assets, 90% of the takings as dividends must be disbursed to investors in terms of the entity getting any potential Internal Revenue Service tax benefits, and 95% of revenue has to be passive (Chen, 2021b).

Tony DiPietro explains,

Another means of earning additional income can be investing in real estate. One can invest directly in physical real estate by the ownership of real property. This would require an investment of capital to purchase a house, maybe make some improvements, and sell it for a profit. It can also include purchasing a house and renting it to tenants for an income stream. Owning real property can be costly and time consuming, but it can be an investment that grows over time.

Being an owner of real property or investment properties does involve risk, and one should consider one's financial situation when deciding if this a suitable investment. For example, one can purchase a property and after investing in improving it, the value of the market could change so that one may not be able to sell the property for what one invested in it. The rental market could decline and rent prices could fall, or one may have a tenant who loses their job and cannot pay the rent. These are some possibilities and risks associated with the direct purchase and management of physical real estate.

One can also invest indirectly through the purchase of a real estate investment trust, also known as a REIT. A REIT is a fund in which investors can purchase shares of a real estate portfolio, and in return, if the value of that portfolio increases along with the rental income produced by that portfolio increasing, they would share in the capital appreciation and profits without the physical management of the real property. On the other hand, the value of holdings or rental income could decrease which can create a risk to an investor and lead to the loss of one's initial investment.

As mentioned throughout this section, each investment does have an element of risk and the possibility of losing one's initial investment, so one should consider one's personal and financial situation before deciding if an investment is suitable. Nonetheless, having the knowhow and experience is imperative, and at any rate, one does have a myriad of options in terms of real estate investment including the high-end luxury type of real estate investment for those who are experienced and have been in the game for a while.

Maria Wood, Luxury Real Estate Broker Associate and REALTOR® with Keller Williams Legacy Realty. Sales and Marketing Coordinator for Luxury Custom Home Builder, Landmark Custom Builder & Remodeling in Kissimmee, FL. explains,

> I am often asked whether it is a good time to invest in real estate, what are the different types of real estate investments, and how to get started. During my career in the real estate industry, I have helped countless individuals and families from all walks of life and from all different cultural and religious backgrounds start or add to their real estate portfolio. Most people have similar goals in mind and have asked themselves these questions:
>
> *"What can I invest in that will maintain or increase in value over time?"*
>
> *"What kind of investment can be passed on to my children?" (Generational Wealth)*
>
> *"What investments have the opportunity to create passive income?"*
>
> *"Which investment allows me to enjoy benefits from it now?"*
>
> Firstly, you do not need to be a millionaire to invest in real estate. There are many creative financing options available if you do not have the cash right now.
>
> Secondly, it is ALWAYS a good time to invest in real estate. The market ebbs and flows: sometimes it is a buyer's market, and sometimes it's a seller's market, but in both markets transactions are happening and rentals are always in demand.
>
> Thirdly, find a licensed REALTOR® (Member of the National Association of REALTORS®) to help guide you on your real estate adventures. You can search www.realtor.com to find one in your area that specializes in the property type you are interested in (Residential, Commercial,

Business Brokerage, Property Management, etc.). There is no reason for a Buyer to attempt to research and negotiate real estate transactions on their own, especially when it costs them little to nothing for an Agent's expert services. In most cases the Agent is paid by the Seller, so save yourself time and frustration and let a professional assist you whether buying, selling, or leasing.

And PLEASE respect and be loyal to your Agent. This career is not as easy as it looks and by all means if you are interested in this career, you should take the pre-license course and state exam and start your own business. You will find Agents have invested many years into their training, licenses, and continuing education. Agents will invest countless hours researching property for you, driving all around showing property, often weekends away from their own families in an attempt to make a living by helping their customers. The most disrespectful thing you can do if you want to be involved in real estate, is to use someone for their time and information, and then switch to another agent, (or your friend or family member who just got their license) for the sale. On behalf of all real estate professionals, PLEASE do not do this and THANK YOU! Home inspectors, appraisers, community association managers and Boards, construction workers, property managers, Real Estate Agents, landscapers, pool technicians, security guards and cleaners all play an important role in the success OR failure of your real estate endeavors!

Important: Discuss with your Agent what your investment goals and needs are. Discuss what your current asset portfolio looks like, what are your current liabilities, what are your upcoming cash needs such as retirement or college, what is your risk level or comfort level, must the property have earning potential, your ability to self-manage or handle maintenance, the time required by you the investor and the tax implications. Keep in mind Real Estate has a low liquidity compared to savings accounts, meaning it takes time to sell at the highest price, and is not the best plan in the event you need cash right away. Help them help you find the appropriate property for your needs if you are the buyer.

Different Types of Real Estate Investing Can Include:

The Residential Single-Family Home: This is the most traditional investment, and one I recommend everyone participate in. I'm going to speak about this category the most as it is my area of expertise. The home you and your family live in is the most important investment you can make, not only financially, but for the benefit of your family and the potential for passing on to your heirs.

Single Family Home for Flipping: You and a couple investors/friends/relatives along with a Real Estate Agent and contractor can find a small starter home with "good bones" in an up-and-coming neighborhood. Have the contractor assist with quoting repairs and arranging the tradespeople who will be doing the work unless you are handy enough to do it yourself! Some things should always be handled by a licensed professional so don't cut corners! Remodeling kitchens, bathrooms, flooring and paint with yield the most return on your investment. Have your Real Estate Agent re-list the property and sell it for a profit. If you are really experienced at doing this, then you can get into buying tax deeds and property auctions. This can also be a condominium, townhouse or mobile home.

Single Family Home for Lease: After the above steps are completed, instead of selling, ask your Real Estate professional if they handle property management. Anyone claiming to be a property manager (of other people's property), MUST have an active real estate sales license and work under a Real Estate Broker (in Florida at least). You can check for licenses by searching the Department of Business and Professional Regulation website. Do not let an inexperienced, unlicensed person manage and maintain what could be one of your largest investments.

With the high cost of buying a home and the high rental rate of apartment complexes, renting a home will ALWAYS be in demand. Families looking for more bedrooms, yards, pools, good schools, will be lining up to rent. Oftentimes several students will rent together if near a college or several friends will share the rent. A good property manager will handle the tenant phone calls, repairs, replacements, advertising, background checks and collect payments.

Certain communities especially where I am near Orlando theme parks, are zoned for short term rental. Again, hire a trusted property management company who does this professionally. When leasing, factor in any membership dues and the Homeowners Association fees which can be quite high in some areas, especially if it is a condominium. Typically, there is a nightly rate that changes based on season, and most folks who own in a vacation destination area also use the property as a second home for their family and friends. I have even helped investors build and buy large 10-13 bedroom mansions, for the purpose of short term rental. "Who rents these places?" I have seen large families come down with rooms for the Grandparents and themed rooms for the grandkids, Sports Trips such as Golfers, Cheerleaders in town for a competition, and Baseball spring training groups. I have seen religious groups come down for their holidays. CEOs bring top managers down for a business meeting/retreat. Women's groups, doctors' groups, couples' retreats, I even attended a destination wedding and reception in one of these homes. Even with the pandemic, folks were here in Orlando working from home and home schooling in the Florida sun. This is the future of travel. As folks are weary of large crowds, cooking at home in a gourmet kitchen, watching a movie in the home theater and entertaining themselves in the in-home bowling alley or Turkish Spa have become all the rage! Keeping the family together and safe, and the environment clean are the priorities of today's traveler.

"Are they making a profit?" In short, YES. There are many factors that determine income. Be wary of anyone offering to predict how much you will generate in positive cash flow. I do in fact know owners who have done very, very well, who are very happy with their rate of return, and who could tell you the methods they have used. How great to get your expenses paid and, in many cases, generate passive income, and create generational wealth!

BY SCOTT GLENN

Other Types of Real Estate Investing:

Multi-Family Units, Apartments or Duplex: Owning one building, and collecting rental income from several units or apartment. Drawbacks include a higher cost for the building and higher reserves needed for repairs, possibly paying a maintenance staff.

REITS = Real Estate Investment Trusts: Are companies that own or finance income producing real estate. They provide investors with long term capital appreciation, diversification in their portfolio, and regular income streams.

Commercial Property: Investment Real Estate Brokers have additional knowledge to serve their commercial investors. Office buildings, strip malls, free standing stores, and restaurants are the most common. The downside would be large initial investment or high rent, remodeling, calculating consumer traffic and location feasibility. Consult your Commercial/Investment Real Estate Agent on terms such as Gross Lease, Net Lease, Escalator Lease, Index Lease, Pro Rata expenses, Capital Expenditures, Capitalization Rate, Equity Dividend Rate, etc.

Vacant Land: Investing in vacant land can be one of the least expensive ways to start investing. Anything from a lot in a growing neighborhood up to several acres of wooded areas or farmland for future growth would be a good place to start. Always do your "due diligence" and check with the HOA if applicable, City and County for zoning ordinances, wetlands, builder rights, and surrounding areas to buy land with the best and highest possible use. Often land purchases need to be cash purchases or a private lender as it is difficult to find a land lender/land loan.

Business Brokerage: Business Brokerage is not only about buying a building like a restaurant building. Instead, in most cases, you are buying everything: from the building to the established brand, the customers, and the reputation of the business. Find a Business Broker who specializes in analyzing the business data, and it can be an effective way to jump right into an existing business model.

However, you start, whatever you do, do not be scared. Consult a CPA and attorney for advice; you don't have to guess or do everything alone! Open an LLC (Limited Liability Company), for tax benefits and legal protection. Develop relationships with mortgage lenders and private equity investors who can assist you in reaching your goal. Find someone who is doing what you would like to be doing and learn from them! Time and time again Real Estate has proven to be one of the safest and most reliable forms of investing!

REIT Negatives and Positives

Risk occurs in any type of investment; it just depends on one's action in terms of investing. Barbara Friedberg (2021d) says that REIT revenues have the potential drop when interest rates are high and fewer people are taking out mortgages. High interest rates also make financing real estate more expensive and cause borrowers to have to pay more interest. Dividends are good, but one will have to pay taxes on dividends, usually at a higher rate than the 15% imposed on nearly all dividends since most REIT earnings are regarded as ordinary income, though this differs by the REIT.

Some of the main positives in terms of REITs are that they have a long history of growing their dividends, the properties owned by REIT firms can grow in worth in the future which expands one's original investment, they are efficiently managed to get good returns on the individual properties, they offer diversification to securities within a portfolio, which restricts losses if other investments drop in value, and they are simple to purchase and sell by way of one's electronic investment account. In general, one can expand one's invested assets but must keep in mind the importance of comprehending which will be prosperous and which will not. If one's REITs are not the greatest investments for a few years, in the long term, they are a sound investment in terms of real estate and can expand one's financial worth (Friedberg, 2021d).

CHAPTER 9

INVESTMENT POTPOURRI: THE SWEET SMELL OF SUCCESS FROM ALTERNATIVE INVESTING SOURCES

Thus far, I have explained the general common or known manner in which to invest. In this chapter, I will cover less common ways of investing for tomorrow by way of crowdfunding, flipping websites, cryptocurrency, and commodities of various types.

Crowdfunding and Platforms

Back in the day, if one wanted to raise money for something, one had to go to the bank. Technology places access to cash and funding at one's fingertips by way of the internet with the use of crowdfunding which can be beneficial in terms of cost as well as efficient in terms of time. One must comprehend that not all of these platforms of funding provide the same advantages.

Loan crowdfunding involves borrowing funds on an individual-to-individual basis. As long as one does not run a lending business, this type of funding is not highly regulated. To receive this funding, one needs to reveal one's own financial status, and if one is lending the funds, this action can be risky because of the lack of regulation. The receiver of the loan is responsible for seeing that the funds are reimbursed. The lender should keep in mind that restricting the amount and extent of the loan is important and ensure that the return is worth the risk. Another good source of crowdfunding is the donation route which, in most cases, is for a cause but sometimes to start a business. This sort of funding requires an "eyecatcher" type of motivational story that inspires people to contribute, and one does not have to reimburse the funding.

Exchange crowdfunding is requesting funds for one's business and then after developing a product or meeting some goal, giving the funder the product which is usually equivalent to or more than the original funding. This funding is without regulation, and the funds do not have to be reimbursed. Once the product is finished, those who funded the product receive the product, but sales tax may be the developer's responsibility. If one provides the funding, one must remember that if the product is unsuccessful or the business goes under, one's money may never be recovered.

Finally, equity crowdfunding involves selling a share (stock) in one's business. The legality of this type of funding is presently under review. Once regulations are in place, it would be important to have a lawyer to oversee this type of funding (*Four Kinds of Crowdfunding*, n.d.). Crowdfunding is somewhat complicated but can be advantageous if one has the knowledge. This type of funding can be delivered by way of a website which is another method to make cash.

Flipping Websites

One may have heard of flipping houses in the real estate business, and it may appear to look easy after viewing various shows on television. Rodley (2021) defines website flipping as putting time and money into websites that already are profitable or making them better by growing the number of visitors to the site or making more money from the same number of visitors and then selling the site to make money. Profile Tree (n.d.) says that what one may not be aware of is the ability to buy and/or flip websites is easier to get involved in than many other types of investment because it needs less capital.

Website flipping evolved from the housing market in terms of flipping houses where a businessperson would seek an entity that was not doing well and buy it. The businessperson would use their experience and expertise to make the business better and then sell it for a good price. In addition, the price paid will be contingent upon how much income the present holder will spend by giving up control of the site. Although flipping websites may be of great interest to some, much investigation into the matter is necessary so that time and money are not wasted. The internet business is huge, and although very prosperous, most of the ecommerce sites are not very good in terms of attracting people.

One must keep in mind that the cash one can get from a site depends on the condition the site is in when one acquires it. Understanding what is considered a good site to flip and having the expertise and ability is key. Website Builders (2020) explains that one can construct and sell a fresh website or, like a house, flip one that is already in order. Constructing a website is somewhat like constructing a home; one chooses a spot and what will be built there and starts the work. When one purchases a website that is not operating up to par, one changes the website to make it profitable and sells it.

Rodley (2021) explains that creating a website from the start involves realizing a lucrative specialty, using WordPress, choosing a traffic-making tactic, putting in an outstanding search engine optimization, and then converting traffic flow on the website to cash. In terms of purchasing an existing site, one should pick a site that clearly proves the concept works, determine the website's potential for growth, improve the site, and sell it. Flipping web sites and crowdfunding may be uncommon ways of making money, but not like the wonder of cryptocurrency and the assorted ways to use commodities.

Cryptocurrency

Cryptocurrency is a curious attraction in the investment world. It is not government controlled and is exchanged by way of technology. Cryptocurrency dates back to the 1970s and is known for its various forms including the most popular Bitcoin (Lee, 2021). In mid-2021, one Bitcoin was valued close to $55,000. If one had invested in Bitcoin when it first started in 2009, one would have great wealth today. Years ago, this cryptocurrency was just an academic hypothetical notion, but through the years leading up to contemporary days, the investment idea is realistic and happening regularly globally (Lee, 2021). Cryptocurrencies are all electronic exchanges and there are no physical transfers. All exchanges come from a technological file by way of virtual trade. These currencies can also be delivered and held electronically on a computer hardware apparatus like a backup drive and not "Uncle Sam." Cryptocurrency imparts money as well as securities making it unclear which one it truly is. Buying clout with cryptocurrency is limited as this type of currency is not received by firms. In addition, perceiving it as an investment is kind of shaky as well since it is not particularly like conventional investment securities but more like commodities (discussed next) that can be purchased and sold for monies as well as byproducts centered on anticipated upcoming worth.

The term cryptocurrency stems from the actual ways in which the system is safeguarded making use of blockchains that ensure the reliability of exchangeable information. Many experts think these blockchains will disrupt the world of industry, finance, and law (Frankenfield, 2021). The government does not back cryptocurrencies unlike most traditional currencies (Little, 2021). Cryptocurrencies are criticized for their "illegal activities, exchange rate volatility, and vulnerabilities of the infrastructure underlying them" (Frankenfield, 2021, para 4).

Commodities

A commodity can be perceived as a tangible good that can be bought and sold or traded for other goods of similar worth. Goods like oil and basic foods like corn are commodities. These commodities can be exchanged on the market like regular securities and can also alter in price according to supply and demand (Maffatt, 2019).

When it comes to investments, commodities are often disregarded with an emphasis on investing in regular securities such as stocks and bonds. Commodities like silver and gold, oil, and farming commodities operate according to supply and demand in their individual industry environment and can be very alluring when it comes to a diversified portfolio (Royal, 2021a). There are different ways of investing in commodities. One can invest in commodities directly or by way of mutual funds and ETFs, and with future agreements (Kowalski, 2021). Fidelity Learning Center (2021) explains that investing in commodities can be done in different ways such as buying assorted sums of objective raw materials, futures contracts, and mutual funds but can bring about different returns when one or the other does better. Royal (2021a) explains a few ways to invest in commodities.

Stock of commodities producers is another way to invest if one does not want to physically purchase commodities but wants to invest in the producers of commodities. As the price goes up on the commodity, that entity usually gets a return as well as potential growth in production in the future, creating more revenue. The negative aspect of this type of investment is that the investment is definitely high risk because of uncertain ups and downs in the producer's economic situation along with these firms requiring extensive capital.

Purchasing commodities by way of the futures market is a well-known method, but it is very risky and therefore has a greater return on investment. Commodities are known as futures because exchanges are not made for immediate delivery but for later because time is needed for that particular commodity to be cultivated, reaped, mined, or refined (Maffatt, 2019).

One can build cash fast, but the antithesis is that one can lose it fast as well. One can also own physical commodities such as silver and gold directly to defend against inflation, purchasing them via online dealers or pawn shops. The disadvantage with this type of investment is that silver and gold may be stolen; therefore, one must ensure that these valuables are insured. In addition, when selling the coins, silver, or gold, it can be difficult to obtain their true value.

ETFs of physical commodities enable one to own commodities by way of technology (ETFs) on the futures market instead of the physical route. One could purchase an ETF that possesses silver or gold or a mix of goods which is advantageous because it gives one exposure to the commodity goods as well as market-based pricing, allowing one to receive the best price for the goods when one wants to sell them. The downside to this avenue of investing is that ETFs expose one to the fluctuating prices of the goods.

Diversity in terms of investments is always ideal. Royal (2021a) further explains that another avenue to acquiring diversified exposure to commodities producers is to purchase an ETF that owns an assortment of them. A good diverse mix is preferable in commodity investments but is not a definite guarantee in terms of losses. Exchange rates, inflation, supply and demand, and the economic well-being of the nation play a vital role in causing commodity prices to go up and down. The worldwide infrastructure today has risen in demand due to ventures and undertakings abroad, and an upsurge in commodity prices will hopefully have a profound bearing on stocks within firms in associated industries.

Inflation can lower the worth of an entity's securities such as in stocks and bonds which can be beneficial for commodities as prices go up and commodities perform well, but the drawback is that commodities can be a lot more volatile than other securities. People who invest in commodities could lose their investment due to the effects of global action, international competition, government parameters, and economic environments (Fidelity Learning Center, 2021). Overall, commodities are prevalent these days as a shield against inflation, the performance of commodities is not as tied to regular investing securities like stocks and bonds which helps in diversification, and they help to circumvent other risks within one's assorted investments. One must keep in mind that while there are many ways to trade in commodities, it is imperative to be knowledgeable about the positives and negatives of the investment, no matter the method used. Also, high prices in most cases are short-lived, making commodities a less likely investment (Royal, 2021a).

Commodities are goods that are made and sold by many different companies, but there is uniformity in quality between the companies that make and sell them. Commodities like corn and oil are perfect examples, but natural gas is not because it is too costly to transport internationally although can be traded in certain areas. Diamonds also do not fit the bill in terms of investment in commodities because they differ too much in value to acquire the volumes of scale needed to sell them as classified commodities (Maffatt, 2019).

Benefits of Investing in Commodities

The benefits of investing in commodities are several. Maffatt (2019) explains that trading in commodities permits cultivators and manufacturers to get their disbursements as an early payment, providing them with liquid capital add to their entity, take profits, reduce debt, and increase production. Investors also benefit because they can benefit from the declines in the market to enhance their assets (Maffatt, 2019). Wong (2015) explains that exposure to diverse growth opportunities is an advantage of investing in commodities. Historically, they have shown a low correlation to securities like traditional stocks and bonds which makes commodity investments a good hedge against stock and bond investments. They also provide protection against inflation (Wong, 2015).

Liabilities of Investing in Commodities

The liabilities or risks of investing in commodities stem from the enormous volatility mainly in terms of future agreements (Kowalski, 2021). Dummies (n.d.) says that "there is also a geopolitical danger with investing in commodities. One of the inherent risks of commodities is that the world's natural resources are located in various continents and the jurisdiction over these commodities lies with sovereign governments, international companies, and many other entities" (p.1). The natural resources globally can have a profound impact on one's choice to invest in commodities. The attitudes of governments as well as the entities that are in business have to be taken into consideration, and international differences in terms of who has control of the resources are frequent. In addition, traders in commodities markets, as in other markets, seek short-term earnings by speculating whether prices will go up or down, so one needs to learn to be aware of speculators. Finally, there is the risk of fraud in trading commodities (Dummies, n.d.). Wong (2015) states that although commodities can be an advantage to one's portfolio, these investments can be twice as volatile as stocks and four times as volatile as bonds. In addition, unlike most other assets, commodities do not generate income for the investor.

People may wonder if traditional securities like stocks and bonds are better than alternative investments or should be included in their portfolio. Most individuals see investment as just regular securities and stocks and bonds and the only way to invest. The answer is for one to determine one's objectives early in terms of time and actual assets and financial situation and consider these factors in creating one's portfolio. Afterwards, one can assess what one wants in one's portfolio with an idea of a potential mix of conventional securities and alternative investments. One can have a better investment if one includes a particular ratio and variety of investments such as real estate including REITs as well as stock and bond securities (Retire Certain, n.d.). Cryptocurrency, flipping websites, commodities, and other alternatives can add to one's portfolio if proper research and planning are implemented, but understanding business in all its forms and entrepreneurship is important for all of the investments we have discussed thus far as well as for reducing the wealth gap.

THE POWER OF KNOWLEDGE: COMPREHENDING HOW ENTREPRENEURSHIP AND BUSINESS PLAY A ROLE IN INVESTMENT

Chapter 10 is the longest chapter in the book, and it could have been the first due to the importance of understanding what business and entrepreneurship are and how they are related to investing. I have put this chapter at the end because, although it is important, the focal point of the book is investment and the importance of being frugal so that one can invest. *Nonetheless, knowledge is power, and one needs to comprehend business and entrepreneurship and how economic activity impacts domestic and global affairs.*

In addition, one should know that a business cannot operate without its people (human relations). Leadership, teamwork, and management are essential for a successful business entity. Business involves including all stakeholders in the triple bottom line (business, society, and environment), understanding various viewpoints is what a true business is all about. Environments are everchanging, and adaptation with sound diversity matters in all walks of life and for all stakeholders. Therefore, one must comprehend Maslow's pyramid of needs so that emotional intelligence is not undermined or totally forgotten in a business. A company's financial reports provide valuable information for investors in terms of the health and well-being of the company. Finally, knowing and comprehending the different types of business and their functions is important as well.

I have always explained to students that business, marketing, and economics are an interrelated family in that they are all clearly tied together. Marketing is the activity of the business while the business which involves customers, supply and demand, and business cycles makes the economy go round. To understand business, one must first consider the definition of the term. Many definitions exist, but one can define business as the engaging practice of activities involving the selling and buying of goods, services, and perhaps even ideas.

The term business is broad and dates back in history to bartering. The concept of bartering is a mutual and coincidental agreement without the use of money which has involved the exchanging of such assets like animals, natural resources, or goods that humans have created or manufactured. Bartering continued through the centuries across the world extending to the Americas including the United States. Although bartering "simmered down" and currency was "invented," bartering still was practiced especially in places and times where money was lacking, as in the United States during the Great Depression. Nonetheless, money remains the overall means of exchange and continues to transform in terms of its delivery and payment.

In current times, the use of innovative technology has evolved, including mobile and virtual forms of payment. This is done electronically by means of computers, cell phones, and other devices for point-of-sale payments. Therefore, in a sense, bartering continues with the use of these technological sophisticated ways of exchanging "things" and money. The internet is important in the exchange of money in terms of trade as well. Today, money can be exchanged internationally as fast as it can locally.

Investment Business Importance: Economics and Activities

Business is what makes the world go round, and business incorporates all the stakeholders who have an impact on the business. As stated above in the introduction, a business can be described as an individual or establishment who seeks to make profit by exchanging products or services in terms of meeting the needs or wants of consumers. Those entities that do not emphasize or primarily seek to earn profit are considered nonprofit entities. No matter the type of business, how the firm is constructed economically is important, and the various business activities that rely on one another in terms of creating customer satisfaction must be done properly to create profits for the firm. Some of the marketing activities include selling, promotion, pricing, distribution, advertising, and researching (primary and secondary), buying behavior and competition along with supply and demand, which is essential. In contemporary business, both domestic and internationally, manufacturing, services, merchandising, and a mix of these and others (hybrid; see Types of Business section below) continue to "make the world spin" with the use of these various activities. These activities come from the power of the people, and their input should not be taken lightly even in this highly technological world of machines.

Human Relations and Human Capital

Human relations can be perceived as the study of people in terms of their behavior and relationships. One cannot help but to add the importance of human capital in terms of relationship with self or others. Therefore, it is important for organizations to continue to research and understand what empowers and motivates people. I explain human capital in the next several paragraphs from pages121-125, in *Personal Finance: An Encyclopedia of Modern Money Management* (Friedberg, 2015) as "the idea that intelligence and skillfulness make humans valuable."

> The notion that the country's prosperity is exemplified in its people was initially expressed in the United States of America at the start of the 20th century. By the end of the century, the world acknowledged that academia is important for technology implementation as well as economic expansion (Goldin, 2002). The debate on human capital continues, and its focus is changing from physical aspects to human facets. As research and theories continue to evolve, some questions may arise. Perhaps, businesses may have overlooked or underestimated the power of human capital, and with contemporary exposure, maybe,

human capital will override the strength of physical capital. This question is evident: Can the business world and other entities achieve a sound balance in terms of implementing both physical and human capital within their business realms?

Even though this idea of human capital has been noted dating back to the 1900s, the notion of human capital can be traced back to the 1600s. In about 1691, Sir William Petty put worth on workers and assessed the worth of human capital to show the strength of England and appraised the price of lives taken by way of warfare and other deaths. In 1853, William Farr described the current worth of an individual's net future profits as profits minus living expenditures. He claimed that net future profits signified prosperity in the same way as material possessions and ought to be taxed in the same way.

In 1867, Theodore Wittstein said that Farr's current worth of net future profits ought to be used in courts of law to decide reimbursement for requests in terms of life that has been taken away. In 1930, two businessmen who dealt in insurance, Alfred Lotka and Louis Dublin, tried to use Wittstein's idea to determine the quantity of life insurance that a person should buy. They went beyond Wittstein's current worth of net future profits to contemplate death statistics (Kiker, 1966).

Human capital was emphasized in the business world during the 1950s and 1960s when labor economists started to study labor force quality. Businesses spent money on training and academic education in the hope of enhancing efficiency as well as incomes. After these pioneers of human capital, various other people added to the idea of human capital in terms of economics by considering the ways that people are thought of as an investment which brings forth a return. Many others also acknowledged the idea but did not want to perceive people in the same way as physical commodities because of sentimentalism (Berry, 2007).

Throughout the decades, the claim of what is known as human capital theory has been employed to tackle matters pertaining to civic courses of action, and many

MONEY HAS NO COMPLEXION

of these situations are still the focus of the theory in contemporary days. Such topics include the influence of countries, the outcomes of migration, investments in as well as supervision of well-being, well-being investing, economic expansion and academic procedure and investing. Human capital economics, like other sciences, is not immobile but continues to progress, and during any period, it is the product of what occurred beforehand (Kiker, 1966). Schulz (n.d.) notes in his essay on human capital that in striving to calculate the importance of human capital, economists have estimated the whole stock of human capital in the United States of America at more than $700 trillion, way above the physical capital stock of $45 trillion.

Becker Murphy (2007) maintained that greater rates of return on capital signify higher production in the economy. This statement is totally valid for both human capital and physical capital. The primary effect of greater returns to human capital is broader inequity in terms of wages, but young people may reverse this inequality as time goes by investing more in their human capital.

Schrange (2012) provides a wider viewpoint, stressing how inspiring creativity signifies a special type of human capital investment that is currently not noticed. He says that innovators' main assets may not be their workers, but their consumers. What is important is investing in the consumer, which involves raising the consumer's proficiency level. Perhaps, these aspects are what decide whether an entity is going to prosper. Schrange continues that human capital of the consumer plays a vital role in a business and that increasing the human capital of consumers and clientele is as cost-effective, fiscally sound, and tactically imperative as overseeing the human capital proficiencies of the firm. Innovation creates an innovative prosperity in terms of human capital. Consumers and clients obtain new abilities and new communication standards, leading to an increase in value.

Formal economic theory as well as empirical study have regrettably undermined and belittled the importance of the consumers' human capital in innovation achievement. Fruitful innovators have indulged in quality and quantity simultaneously, and this intertwining of the two has created an upsurge in human capital stock of their consumers and clients. This is proof that their success is due to their innovations making their consumers and clients indispensable (Salam, 2012).

The importance of businesses is currently being emphasized in many ways, and research demonstrates that businesses that move from a status of above average to superior do so because of the qualities and emphasis that they place on the workers themselves through the all-inclusive business entity which involves leadership. Fortune's *America's Most Admired Companies* is an exclusive list because ranking depends on perception of human capital as the top aspect. These companies emphasize worker aptitude, management quality, and origination and civic obligation. The focal theme is that investors and business personnel love entities who give prominence to the human capital facets of their entity (Phillips, 2005).

The importance of human capital in comparison to physical capital will continue to be a controversial issue in America. A question that people will continue to ask is this: If all American business entities incorporated an identical model in terms of the amounts of all measured input including human capital so that equality of work is acknowledged, would this action be considered a fair practice or a socialistic situation?

Human capital starts with the individual (human personal capital) perception and the way they view their most basic needs. Maslow's pyramid is great theory in terms of meeting human needs with the five basic needs seen as physiological, security, social, esteem, and self-actualization. This theory demonstrates that human behavior can be motivated by way of manipulation or empowerment with the latter being the best way. Such action as behavior modification can have negative and positive effects. Rewarding is good, but punishment may have long-term negative effects on behavior, causing discontented mindsets towards work and a revolving door in terms of exiting the organization. Those establishments that understand their people while meeting the mission, vision, and goals of the organization will have more success. This requires businesses to be able to adapt and become flexible so that employee needs and, in some cases, wants are taken care of. The desired use and employment design depend on the people and the organization. Therefore, sound management is needed.

Management

The economy trickles down to a business and all stakeholders tied to it (see paragraph below). Management is a broad term and in general is includes upper management who create the strategic planning, intermediate management who oversee the separate operations commanded from the top, and the supervisors who oversee the employees each day. One must comprehend that the structure or hierarchy of an entity in terms of management may differ from business to business. Management is an important part of any entity and can be generally perceived as guiding an organization in terms of organizing, planning, maintaining, empowering, and motivating, adapting, and changing various aspects with efficiency and effectiveness so that the mission, vision, and goals are met. Or one can simply say, "taking care of the entity and it's people!" In an everchanging diverse world, managers need solid intellect and technical, analytical, and conceptual abilities to empower and motivate employees while delegating assignments in a proper manner. One must remember that delegation, at every level of management, involves outstanding communication and emotional intelligence which entails proper listening throughout the organization and ensuring processes are ethical.

Ethics and Social Responsibility: The Triple Bottom Line and '96'

I have taught many ethics classes at the college and university level as well as writing a book on the topic. The general definition of ethics is the morals, values, or principles of a person or people involving what is right and wrong in terms of how they act in the various components in life. We are who we are due to how we were raised, our religious experience or lack of it, and life experiences in general.

When looking at the numbers 9 and 6, depending which way up one views the numbers, each person will form a different perception, especially if neither has experienced the other perception. On the other hand, because we all are different, some, even if they have experienced the other viewpoint, may want to ignore the viewpoint, and hold on to just what they feel comfortable with or want to believe. In the contemporary world, these principles, morals, and values may come into conflict for these various reasons.

Nonetheless, businesses have a duty or a corporate social responsibility to be ethical these days whether they want to or not. This is especially true for developed countries and world powers like the United States of America. Gone are the days when a firm just focused on revenue and profit without supporting society and the environment. Revenue and profits, societal matters, and the environment are of equal importance, involving all stakeholders, and together, are considered the triple bottom line.

Investment: Stakeholder Importance

Many may view stakeholders as just those who have stock (stock/shareholders) in a company, but this is not the case. Stakeholders are those who may have "a piece" of the firm or those who are simply affected by the firm externally such as the community, the government, and suppliers, to name a few. Remember! Stakeholders can be inside or outside the company (internal and external) and are or can be affected by the firm in many ways.

For example, if a firm is making much revenue but at the same time helping the people in the community (stakeholders) in some way as well as contributing to helping the environment, then this company is contributing positively in terms of the triple bottom line. In turn, positive facets such as the government providing incentives for helping the environment can be delivered. In addition, society will provide that firm with a good reputation which aids in brand awareness. Brand awareness cannot develop or be maintained without proper guidance and leadership which involves sound communication.

Leadership/Teamwork and Communication

A perennial debate is whether leaders are born or made. I think the answer is both. Nonetheless, leadership starts from the top and is a sound reflection on the entire entity, whether it be a country, firm, or even a family. In terms of a business, one can say that a leader needs sound skill to be successful in ensuring that their leadership is guiding an organization in the right direction. Important leadership skills include the skills discussed in the management section (solid intellect, technical, analytical, and conceptual skills, ability to empower and motivate others) along with diversity awareness, thorough communication, and good listening skills. In addition, leaders must display integrity and adopt a leadership style suited to the organization while mentoring and teaching and leading by example. If these aspects are put into place, the teams can be formed and operate accordingly.

In the 2016 Diversity in Ed. Magazine, I wrote an article explaining what leadership is by saying, "demonstrating proper leadership and engagement in sound teamwork while motivating and empowering a team can be contagious throughout the entity. Effective leadership can be viewed as a leader always setting an example in all that they do by communicating properly to bring everyone together while emphasizing the fact that listening to each other is imperative. More important, leaders must truly care for the people they lead. This does not mean a leader is easily manipulated or 'soft.' When leadership is administered the right way, a team or a group can operate effectively and efficiently. A one-size-fits-all approach to teamwork is never suitable for different occasions. Knowing team members both individually and collectively strengthens the team. Comprehending how individuals, groups, and teams are different can enhance the workplace environment. A group can be defined as two or more individuals who correspond with each other and have a common identity and goal. A team is a group of people who have corresponding skills, have a common purpose, goal, and approach, and hold themselves mutually accountable. Leaders should remember that teams are groups of individuals, but not all groups are teams" (p.1-2). Finally, staying positive while motivating and empowering employees aids in bolstering the diversified work environment. This diversified work atmosphere involves diversity in a multitude of ways: different people, places, and situations.

The World of Business: Different People, Places, and Situations

Due to technology and its impact on the information age, communication is enabling businesses to expand at a fast rate, and this is causing competition to be even more extensive throughout the planet. Businesses that just think globally and do not act will not survive in this competitive business world. Therefore, the preparation, experience, knowledge, and ability to go across national borders is important.

Many people think the definition of international business is simple, but such is not the case. Terms like international business, foreign business, globalization, multidomestic company, and international company have separate meanings. For example, one may hear the word foreign and right away assume that the business is across country borders, but this is not always so.

A foreign entity or business is one that operates outside its home market while a global company is a business that seeks to normalize or mix and adapt in operations throughout the world in as many places as possible. A multidomestic company is a business that has ties to many countries who have their own individual marketing strategy that is tailored to that specific country. An international company is one that looks to regulate or combine and adapt in operations or has relations to numerous countries who have their own individual marketing strategy that is personalized to that country. Therefore, the simple definition of an international business would be a business that manages its activities across borders. These activities include such aspects as foreign direct investment, trade, services, franchising, joint ventures, and partnerships of various types. No matter the description, doing business internationally requires an entity to be able to comprehend and adapt and be flexible in the environments abroad.

Environments

As was explained in the previous paragraphs, businesses in this everchanging world must be able to understand, adapt, and be flexible in the environments that exist globally. Internal and microenvironments as well as external and macroenvironments have a profound impact on business functions and operations. Understanding what facets affect a business both internally and externally will aid in the overall business process as companies compete not just against each other but in the difficult environments that they will encounter abroad.

The internal environments, which can be controlled, consist of such facets as the business personnel, operations, financials, and marketing aspects while the microenvironment entails the consumers, marketing intermediaries, products, competition, and suppliers. External and macroenvironments, which are not controllable, include technology, political, cultural, and social conditions, demographics, energy and raw materials, and economic and legal systems. Once the business is domestically set and comprehends the environments abroad, the choice to enter business competition in another country can be decided much better as there are various ways to do so if the top executive leadership believes it is time.

Leadership

My personal leadership style involves three main facets which include leading by example, care/appropriate love, and sound communication which emphasizes listening. However, this definition of leadership does not exist in most businesses, let alone other organizations. The reason is that people are different, and their life experiences cause them to perceive leadership in different ways.

International leadership requires a positive personality, education, experience, and skill sets greater than those of the average leader or domestic business leader who is not accustomed to different people and places and difficult situations. Many times, leaders become accustomed to their personal life experiences which include their upbringing, religion, and culture, giving them the perception that their country's culture is superior to others (ethnocentricity).

"When one considers the various attributes essential in today's increasingly global business environment, several qualities 'immediately come to mind: communication skills, Interpersonal skills, and the ability to adjust to different cultural settings" (Gomnior and Richards, 1992, p.3).

Therefore, along with the abilities I have already described, international leaders— and indeed, all leaders—need to be proficient, effective, efficient, and patient. They must be professionally persistent, aware of their strengths, weaknesses, threats, and opportunities (SWOT), modest yet positively confident (knowing their job and themselves), and respectful of culture and diversity. They need to be innovative and have a sound overall global intellect with the ability to strategize, adapt, and be flexible. When business leaders have these qualities and prepare staff soundly and appropriately to do business abroad, then entering any market is not as difficult.

Globalization and Investment

Once the home business is soundly established, the idea of accessing more revenue and growth may be a consideration. There are several ways that a company can enter the business world abroad, and all have assets and liabilities. Doing business abroad, as was discussed earlier in the chapter, requires a sound team of experts with experience, education, relational corporate ties in the countries that the entity is interested in, and thorough research. Licensing, foreign direct investment, wholly owned subsidiary, joint venture, exporting, and franchising are the major ways that companies become involved overseas, and these models branch off into other opportunities as well as other types of investment opportunities.

Once the known means of business is established abroad, making use of the strategic plan of operation is equally tough in the diverse environments. If equipped, the business can take the opportunities offered by these diverse situations. How a company operates will depend on the type of entity it is. However, no matter what business it is, the supply chain is the main linking factor of the business, and without a thoroughly planned out supply chain, the business cannot exist and thrive. This valuable and important process involves the making of the product or service from the start (raw materials) to selling the finished product to the consumer. This chain has significant parts such as information, procedures, materials, financing, resources, and services that aid in cost reduction if done properly.

Without thorough distribution channels and supply chains, customers' needs will not be met, and the business will be in jeopardy sooner or later. The pandemic of 2020 is a great example of this. Distribution channels within the supply chain are imperative avenue streams that are valuable to a business. Distribution channels can be considered direct as well as indirect. The simplest of the two would be direct distribution in which the product is delivered straight to the consumer while indirect distribution involves a "middle" entity such as other business or intermediaries and in most cases is more expensive. Some examples of "middle" entities are distributors, wholesalers, and retailers, each of whom can be tied to the use of technology. Due to the fast pace of the world, the internet itself is considered a distribution channel, and because of the web and its diverse input, the comprehension of different people, places, and situations is essential.

The supply chain operation is critical, and other decisions such as outsourcing or gaining goods and services from an outside supplier can become political in the decision-making process such as deciding to make use of offshoring or taking some of the entity's services, methods, or procedural measures abroad to be cost effective.

Marketing is a broad term that can be defined as activities within a business such as the selling, promotion, and advertising of products and services to meet the needs and wants of consumers. Within the business mission and goals, these activities can be successful if customers are provided with a good experience and outstanding value. If marketing activities are done in the right manner, before, during, and after sales, a bond or relationship can be established which may turn into consumer equity or even a business brand name.

Comprehending Wants and Needs

When taking into consideration the wants and needs of consumers, one must remember the earlier discussion of Maslow's theory or pyramid which considers the needs of a person from most to least essential (discussed earlier in the Business section). To understand these aspects, the use of marketing research is an important factor that must be taken seriously to meet the needs and wants of the consumer. Research is an extensive process and can be done in numerous ways in which two main general approaches are used, primary and secondary research.

Primary research costs more because the data must be gathered by such means as interviews, surveys, observations, focus groups, emails, questionnaires, telephone calls, and face-to-face consultations. Secondary research uses data that has already been collected and is ready for use. Once the research is done, a sound marketing mix, strategy, and plan must be implemented which involves providing the consumer with an experience that is attractive so that it positions the product or service in the mind of the consumer.

Mix---------Strategy----------Plan

The marketing mix is composed of place, price, production, and promotion (4 Ps) and is the most important aspect of a marketing activity, with the product being most important. Place, promotion, and price cannot be of any value or use without the product itself. These four elements that compose this mix construct a sound strategy supported by a thorough plan.

Some view strategy and plan as the same and do not understand their differences, so a simple explanation follows. One way to view a strategy is as the total plan for marketing a product or service to appeal to customers, including the business proposition and research used to target consumers. The plan can be considered the detailed activities that will be used over a period. For example, a football team's play book would be the strategy that will be used throughout the season with a set formation, but the actual plays (plan) may differ from week to week depending on the competition. The play book is the overall long strategy, and the actual plays are the plans that will be utilized according to the team's needs throughout the season.

The marketing plan is a mere way of specifically outlining the marketing strategy within a business. General facets included within the plan are what the company's present position is as well as the marketing goals. The vision, mission, and goals are imperative within the supply chain and distribution channel from start to finish.

Importance of Diversity: Empowering Different People, Places, and Situations

The general systems theory and interactive social system have been mentioned throughout this book as a good example of why people need to work together. The model below demonstrates the general systems theory, interactive social system, diversity, motivation (empowerment) and discipline, and teamwork with appropriate leadership.

Diversity is a wide-ranging term that can involve many aspects. When the word diversity is mentioned, one can think of variety or difference. In terms of business, one can include different people, places, and situations that make up an entity empowered by people and innovative ideas and abilities from abroad. A diverse workforce with skill sets and input from people with different backgrounds can be a positive for an organization. Many organizations have a diverse workforce, but they do not necessarily include those from different cultures or backgrounds in decision making or other processes. Diversity and the inclusion of all people, no matter their culture, religion, ethnicity, special needs, or gender, is important in terms of being represented at the workplace as the United States and the world continue to change at a fast rate. Practicing and implementing diversity within the hiring processes, training, and professional development, and having a truly diverse board is important for those organizations that want to provide equal opportunity and avoid discrimination. Practicing diversity helps an organization to be successful in meeting its mission, goals, and vision supported by a diverse environment with satisfied stakeholders. Yes, understanding diversity at every level helps the business, especially in dealing with the financials and accounting processes, both domestic and internationally.

Comprehending Accounting and Financial Statements

Accounting involves the calculating, recording, summarizing, and communication of financial transactions. This communication is transformed into financial statements that are used internally as well as externally. Financial statements are completed internal to the firm and are used to explain and control the firm's performance so that preparation and direction can be implemented for future aspects and goal setting about the firm. External entities, such as government entities, suppliers, investors, business and market analysts, customers, and lenders, also make use of this information.

For general purposes, I will review the main financial statements starting with the balance sheet. As the saying goes, a picture is worth a thousand words; the same holds true in terms of the information in the balance sheet. The balance sheet includes an overall statement of the condition of the firm, no matter what type of business it is (see Types of Business section below). The income statement explains the organization's profits and losses or revenues and expenses during a specific time.

The cash flow statement gathers the cash earnings and costs and remaining change in cash from the total sum of the organization's operations, financing actions, and investments during a specific time. Other general proforma documents such as the 10-K, 8-K, and 10-Q should also be understood by investors so that they can have a clear picture of the company they are investing in. The 10-K document is used to examine the entity's financial performance annually in the 4th quarter for company stakeholders who are invested. Such items as mentioned above, financial information and statements, management risks, and examination of general business operations are included. This report is mandatory and requested by the SEC. The 8-K is also a valuable document for investors to understand in terms of the corporation's status involving any signs or action that occur and effects the company such as bankruptcy and elections processes.

One can see how this report is valuable in terms of comprehending the "health" of the company and the actions of the people involved. In the 1980-1990s when Apple was evolving, at one point in time, the founder Steve Jobs was fired as the chairman. The company began to go under during the hiatus as a couple chairpersons unsuccessfully took his place. This as well as other data would have been a red flag at the time in terms of investing in Apple.

The 10-Q is also a valuable document in that it provides another financial snapshot of the business's performance and current position. This report is done at the end of each of the four quarters: January-March, April-June, July-September, and October-December.

Financing

Financing is simply managing money and assets so that a person or organization can focus on making a profit while curtailing risks and losses. Therefore, knowing about the organization and estimating whether they can make use of the proper type of financing such as equity or debt financing is important. Business financing is a broad term and includes many different facets. Personal financing involves the individual in terms of his or her own finances. A great personal finance book or encyclopedia to read for overall knowledge with examples would be, as discussed previously, *Personal Finance: An Encyclopedia of Modern Money Management,* edited by Friedberg (2015). Corporate financing and government and public financing are other branches of financing and understanding these is valuable within the business world.

MONEY HAS NO COMPLEXION

Types of Business: Manufacturing, Services, and Merchandise

Manufacturing is the production of various commodities for sale by way of labor or technology after receiving material from a primary production facility to convert it into the final goods. In other words, manufacturing involves obtaining raw materials from a source and then making a product and selling it. Services can simply be described as an intangible action from the business to the consumer. It is intangible in that the service cannot be physically held and is more a performance than an actual physical object. Merchandising is merely the act of fostering the sale of goods or services which are commonly known for retail sale and has become more diverse in terms of the customer experience with the use of technology. A hybrid (mixture) business is also common in the modern world due to rapid demographic changes and demand for customization abroad. Hybrid businesses do not just utilize traditional means and activities but indulge in updated technology so that the customers' needs and wants can be met sooner and more effectively and efficiently. The general types of business are all fitting for investment, but the choice depends on the takers and their economic situation, backgrounds, goals, education, and experience. In terms of ownership, that depends on who is involved and comprehending the various options available.

Entrepreneurship, Small Businesses, and Franchises

Entrepreneurship refers to an approach to business that in many cases is innovative and visionary. One can perceive the entrepreneur as a motivated, controlled, and calculating risk taker who is positively confident, responsible, courageously bold, disciplined, diversified, astute, charismatic, energetic, adaptable, and trustworthy. An entrepreneur is also a problem solver and good communicator.

Many can see various aspects in life, but only a few have vision! Most entrepreneurs see facets that others do not, and at times their idea may even appear somewhat crazy or unrealistic. Nonetheless, the entrepreneur has a driving desire to obtain their idea as the idea remains on their mind constantly. Remember! There is a reason that you have the mental idea so stay with it. What you pursue to do initially in terms of your idea may guide you into something totally different due to your commitment and idea.

Entrepreneurship can start in a personal business, or in some cases, entrepreneurs come from other businesses whether small or large. Entrepreneurs leave these businesses for many reasons and see an opportunity to "chase after" their idea to make their dream become reality. As we learned in the earlier portion of the book, opportunity costs are a constant factor in business just as in life in general. We as people will always have to make decisions, and the tough ones involve trading off or giving up one facet for another.

Rod Robinson, a senior vice president of Insight Sourcing Group leads the firm's Supplier Diversity & Responsible Sourcing Consulting Practice. Prior to joining Insight, Rod was vice president of Supplier Inclusion & Sustainability at Coupa Software. Previous to Coupa, Rod was the founder and CEO of ConnXus, Inc., a cloud procurement platform that enables Global 2000 companies to achieve supply chain objectives related to supply chain transparency, diversity, sustainability, and economic impact. In addition, Rod led the company from start-up through multiple rounds of venture capital financings with 628% revenue growth, building an enterprise customer base including some of the world's leading brands and ultimate acquisition by Coupa Software (Nasdaq: COUP) in 2020.

Rod holds a bachelor's degree in accounting from the West Virginia University Institute of Technology and an MBA from the Wharton School at the University of Pennsylvania. Rod began his career in public accounting as an auditor with Deloitte & Touché where he earned his CPA credentials.

This outstanding entrepreneur tells his story:

> Despite having earned an MBA from Wharton, the world of venture capital was still quite a mystery to me upon graduation over 25 years ago. What I did understand is that venture capitalists made a lot of money by making very risky, early investments in start-up companies founded by visionary entrepreneurs seeking to change the world. By early, I mean before any significant revenue and often before the core product is fully defined. Think Google, Amazon, Facebook, and several more of the world's leading tech companies. Each of these start-ups took venture capital investments to execute visions that would ultimately change the world. It was my own entrepreneurial journey that resulted in my first real education in venture capital.

It was May of 2016 when my team and I announced that we had just closed on a $5 million venture capital investment led by a leading early-stage venture capital firm. I also learned that I was one of a handful of Black start-up founders who had successfully raised over $1million in venture capital. I wasn't sure whether that accomplishment should make me proud or disappointed. What I later learned was that less than 1% of approximately $70 billion in venture capital investments went to Black founders in 2016.

I witnessed, firsthand, what a $5 million infusion capital had just done for my start-up in terms of ability to execute an innovative vision that would ultimately accelerate wealth creation for our diverse employees and investors. More broadly, I had also learned of the enormous returns realized by venture capitalists. For example, I learned (from one of my investors) that an early $50,000 investment in Uber had grown to be worth $700 million by the time they went public. I also learned that a $50,000 angel investment (by a friend) in Zappos grew to a value of $2 million by the time they were acquired by Amazon for nearly a billion dollars. However, I couldn't help but wonder at the volume of wealth creation opportunities being missed due to lack of access to venture capital by founders of color. I was interested in better understanding the reason for this gap in access.

During my capital raising journey, I also realized the absence of investors of color participating as either angel investors or venture capitalists investing in start-ups. While it comes with risk, early-stage venture investment represents one of the greatest sources of wealth creation of our time. Access and knowledge are the key. Whether it's an entrepreneur seeking investment or angel investor looking to invest in the next great innovation, it is important to have access to the right network, access to the right knowledge, and access to the right opportunity. Therefore, I am proud to be associated with the Black Venture Institute, a curriculum-based program dedicated to teaching Black professionals and operators the foundational elements to become angel and venture investors.

BY SCOTT GLENN

Understanding the basic cycle of the entrepreneurial business includes comprehending the S-curve in terms of the company's growth as to anticipation and how to counter various aspects during this very predictable growth. In general, a business may start slow, then pick up tremendously and later fall off. Understanding the S-curve will help a business take care of matters that may negatively or positively affect the business beforehand with strong decision making within the firm and well as externally.

Whatever type of business one partakes in, an outstanding accounting team with sound knowledge is paramount for raising money and financing it. A business idea is great, but one must take heed that the various laws domestically and internationally have a profound impact on a business. Therefore, early in the entrepreneurship stage, it is important to acquire legal advice to protect the entrepreneur, the business, and its intellectual property. The entrepreneur also must consider beforehand how to select a trustworthy, committed, knowledgeable team to support the entrepreneurial idea in developing the business. The people that are chosen should reflect and support the entrepreneur's idea, and they should be as diverse and have as varied experience as possible to get the business well started and to maintain its growth. Somewhere within this formation of the team, the entrepreneur and the management need to construct a thorough business plan and strategy. A basic business plan can consist of the mission, background information, organization, and marketing and financial plans, and an executive summary can be prepared after these aspects are done.

Finally, the entrepreneur and business must ensure that they have the proper technology develop and maintain top-notch services or products. In doing so, the business can grow and compete with other entities domestically or internationally. One must not just think only about the business locally or nationally, but globally as well. Therefore, proper marketing and research must be implemented so that the company can use the information for the good of the business and all stakeholders. One must remember stakeholders are all a part of the triple bottom line! Great examples of entrepreneurs are Steve Jobs and Bill Gates. Although their business at times together was not friendly, they realized that to succeed, they needed to work together and do what was right for the mission at hand.

A franchise, a license to sell another entity's product or service or simply just use their name, can be a sound choice given the right time, place, and business. Most importantly, the franchise must be a brand name with an outstanding business model. The person or people who retain this license and rights are considered the franchisee, and the person or people providing this opportunity are the franchisers. There are some assets as well as liabilities in terms of acquiring a franchise and the pros must outweigh the cons for the licensed business to be successful. The good news is that like any other small business, there are programs such as the Small Business Administration that are available to aid a franchise in terms of valuable information including funding. McDonalds and Subway are two well-known franchises. A business like Starbucks would fall under the corporation business although many may think that it is a franchise. Understanding what these various types of entities are can be important for investors, so let's take a general look at a few such as a sole proprietorship, partnership/limited partnership and LLC, corporation, private/public and initial corporation, joint venture and cooperative, subchapter S corporation and cooperative (co-op), and a nonprofit.

In a sole proprietorship, the most shared type of business establishment in the United States of America, the owner is the man! The woman! The Person! Yet one must understand, businesswise, the proprietor is the only person in control and responsible for the business and all that it entails. A partnership or limited partnership and LLC are two business models that are ideal for small businesses. A partnership involves two or more people connected as co-owners who must comprehend that to operate soundly, written paperwork must be created to hold the individuals accountable. Limited partnership is self-explanatory in which one partner has limited responsibility within the contract. A limited liability company (LLC) is a kind of proprietary that offers restricted commitment and taxation just as a partnership but has fewer limits on associates.

A corporation gets a little more in-depth as there is more responsibility within the company. A corporation is maintained by the invested stakeholders within the entity and separate from the owner. This entity also has paperwork and is guided by the state. On the other hand, a private/public and initial corporation is maintained by just one or a few people who are involved in handling the business which is considered private. This entity involves a company in which anybody can sell, buy, and trade its stock while an initial public offering looks to go public to increase investment and growth.

Quasi-public entities are private and kept by the government to deliver a service. This type of business is focused on providing services to the community and other valuable societal projects. One can also partake in a joint venture which is established for a certain comprehensive development or duration period in which processes are divided equally or one party has more responsibility than the other. A cooperative (co-op), on the other hand, is an association made up of persons or small businesses that have connected to gain the benefits of being tied to a bigger organization. The S corporation can also be beneficial if one wants to be in business. This entity is also taxed like a partnership and LLC in that many stakeholders such as directors, officers, and personnel all partake in the entity.

Finally, a nonprofit in which I have partaken in many forms such as the outstanding Women's Empowerment in Orlando, Florida, concentrates on providing a service rather than receiving a profit and is not maintained by a government entity.

Dr. Cheryl Bowlus, DM, MBAM explains,

> When you are young, have a new business idea that excites you, and cannot wait to make you first million, looking at the elements that are needed to build and sustain a company can be overwhelming. There are many must-do elements to consider, but I am only focusing on two of those important start-up elements. You will find that choosing the right team and putting together a solid financial picture of your company are key components an entrepreneur needs to build a strong organizational foundation.
>
> When the decision to start a new business is made, a new entrepreneur's mine should be filled with the names and credentials of his new team. Recruiting and hiring a strong team can be challenging, but making the wrong choice can bring the company to its knees. The relationships between the team members you hire are serious because the matchups are long-term relationships that are critical to the fluid movement of the company. Young entrepreneurs should see team relationships as the life or death of their company. Building a base that will withstand

the trials and tribulations of the designated industry means bringing together a team that not only have similar thoughts but also have similar values and vision. Assembling a mismatched team without clear ideas can break a young company. Being intentional by listing the qualities and competencies of the new team member before making the choice is important. The decision maker should evaluate their own core competencies, the skills that are needed in others, and the common values they are seeking in new team members. The founder should put a list of filters together then apply them to all candidates. Once the filters are applied, the founder should choose the fit that enhances the values of the company. When an evaluation of all the elements, values, benefits, and analyses has been conducted, choose the new team member, then communicate the mission and vision of the company often. Take your time to hire the new team members but hastily fire those who you realize are a bad fit for the company. The journey to success begins with the right team.

Finding Financial Strength

Evaluating the financial picture of a business is a key element to the success and sustainability of the organization. According to the Small Business Administration (Posell, 2019), not having a well thought out financial plan is a key reason for failure of many start-ups. Putting together the financial plan elements, projected profit-and-loss statement, three-to-five-year projections, cash flow statement, balance sheet, and break-even analysis are critical in establishing the company's financial goals (Chron, 2021). A new business start-up needs to show how and when the money is being spent. Monitoring finances through the financial plan is what is needed to show what went right or what went wrong in the budgeted numbers. New entrepreneurs seeking investment funds are required to know and show the strengths of the company through the financial plan projections. The financial plan, business plan, and marketing strategies should complement each other and lay a strong foundation for the company structure.

An entrepreneur who has a sound financial model is setting their company up with a better chance of succeeding because knowing how, why, and where their money is going means knowing how their money is growing. According to Neil Devani (2021), spending lots of time on financials is not a good thing, but not doing any financials could be a costly mistake. Young start-up company owners should see good financials as the pulse of a good heartbeat. If the beat is bad, the heart will fail. The same goes for a start-up with poor financial planning: "No money = no company" (Devani, 2021, para 4).

Most founders will hand the financial responsibilities to the CFO, but it is important that the young entrepreneur have competencies and skills in financial planning. Young start-up companies will need a strong financial plan during the critical first year of business to make sure they have the key elements to keep the proverbial ship afloat. Knowing how sales forecast and revenue projections affect the company's bottom line are the meat of a good financial plan. The plan plays a significant role in building a stable foundation that can identify growth in a new business. This growth can involve various opportunities including merging with other entities as well as acquiring their assets.

Mergers and Acquisitions

Mergers and acquisitions may seem the same and can be somewhat confusing, but there is a tremendous difference between the two. Mergers involve companies coming together as one, and acquisitions involve one company buying another. There are various types of blends such as vertical, horizontal, and conglomerate mergers. When companies come together who are operating at different but related levels of an industry, it is called a vertical merger. A horizontal merger takes place when businesses produce and sell alike products to the same consumer. Finally, a conglomerate merger involves entities that come together in operation, but their activities are not interconnected.

MONEY HAS NO COMPLEXION

DIVERSIFY INVESTMENT OPPORTUNITIES AND LIMIT LOSSES: CREATING A SHORT- AND LONG-TERM PLAN

Evaluating Investment Opportunities

When assessing an investment, one must first ascertain if the investment is probable in providing the outcome one is looking for grounded on one's general wealth strategy. There are three chief objectives when evaluating investments, and these pertain to income, potential growth in the investment, and capital protection (Retire Certain, n.d.). One must realize that even with sound evaluation and careful tactics, every investment involves some sort of risk. Nonetheless, research needs to be done so that one can get the general information about trading stocks and bonds and other investments. For example, such terms as bull (tendency of increasing prices over time) and bear (tendency of decreasing prices over time) markets need to be understood along with other market investment, business, and financial terms. Various methods have been established to help people to evaluate and choose investments by analyzing market and price variations. Four methods to analyze investments are fundamental analysis, economic analysis, industry analysis, and company analysis.

Fundamental analysis looks at future price movements including financial statistics in a particular company and industry while economic analysis examines the general economic environment including business cycles (ups and downs), inflation, interest rates, and employment rates as well as general growth of the economy. Industry analysis involves considering the life cycle of an industry in terms of high-tech development or altering customer needs and wants and understanding when the industry is at its peak or on the decline. Company analysis is the examination of specific businesses in comparison with similar firms. What pertains to the economy or the industry may not pertain to a specific business (Dorson, 2020). These four concepts are just a few ways to evaluate investments.

Benchmarks for investments like securities, future returns, and real estate are a good instrument for evaluation. Making use of benchmarks, for example, observing the S&P 500 is ideal. As for approximating forthcoming returns within quicker periods, one can view each year independently to decipher how much an investment moved up and down each year historically to get an inkling of how unstable an investment is. In terms of future returns, in the short run, one can observe respective individual years to see how frequently the investment fluctuated annually in the past to comprehend the risk of the investment. Real estate is a little bit trickier, but taking into consideration the "My Look Rule," meaning if the return from leasing the asset is about 10% of the charge of the estate, I will observe further. The reasons that one will want to evaluate investments is to maintain one's objectives, avoid as much risk as possible, take into consideration assessment, time, and cost while answering questions like these: Is the investment worth the risk? Does the investment fluctuate annually? What are the chances of losing everything? (Retire Certain, n.d.).

Assets: Diversify and Allocate While Comprehending Losses and Gains

Having the habit of spreading cash with various investments to aid in lessening risk is diversifying one's portfolio. This diversification in choosing the appropriate investments helps one not to suffer losses and to cut down on the ups and downs of investment yields while at the same time not forfeiting much possible profit.

Implementing asset groups in one's portfolio can aid in balancing out huge loses. Traditionally, the yields of the top asset groups do not fluctuate simultaneously.

One must remember, market circumstances that trigger one asset group to do well, in many cases, cause another to perform not so well or even below par. This is the reason for investing in various asset groups so that one can cut back on investment risks, leveling the playing field in terms of a diversified portfolio.

Asset allocation is also imperative due to the fact that it has a profound impact on whether one meets one's investment objectives. If done properly with knowledge, risky investment can aid in acquiring bigger yields with the inclusion of diverse investments such as stock and stock mutual funds. This all depends on the objectives and goals of the investor, keeping in mind that long- and short-term goals differ in terms of investment and the use of risky investments (Investor.gov, 2021). This long- and short-term investment choice will be discussed below.

Having a plan in terms of investing is imperative, but one should also take note that having a scheme ready just in case losses occur is equally important so that one can pinpoint and settle the matter that triggered one's loss in advance the next time one trades (Mitchell, 2021). One must comprehend that a rebound happens in the natural business cycle or in the national economy's ups and downs. A rebound happens when events, tendencies, or stocks change course and increase following a time of regression. An example would be a company producing strong yields in the fiscal year after the previous year's shortfalls or developing a successful product after previous failures. In reference to the stock market, a rebound is a situation when on a day or for a longer period, a particular stock or the market overall recovers after a decline (Hayes, 2021).

Hicks (2020) offers advice from experienced investors: If one loses assets in the stock market, the best way to recuperate is to get back in the game, and having a diverse portfolio with different investments enables one to even out the portfolio as conditions change in the economy and market. In addition, when the stock market is down, one should think about adding more to one's 401(k) or IRA if possible. By doing so, one is buying extra shares at a better price. Diversifying and allocating one's portfolio is important in order to restrict risk, just as long as one comprehends the various classes and stays engaged (Schwab-Pomerantz, 2021).

M1 Finance is a platform that keeps track of gains and losses to show how investments are performing. M1 Finance (2021) explains that an unrealized gain or loss is a profit or loss which exists in writing in terms of one's investments. One must comprehend that a loss or a gain is realized when it is sold. The formula that helps in terms of calculation is as follows: unrealized gain/loss = value of investment – cost of investment, and unrealized gain/loss % = (value of investment – cost of investment) / cost of investment.

Creating a Short- and Long-Term Plan

When going on a long journey, there is a saying that emphasizes the importance of taking one step at a time and not looking at the top of the stairs. Viewing the entire staircase bottom to top can cause one's focus to stray and create less confidence due to what is seen. Therefore, in terms of personal finance and investing, one should have a short-term plan that leads to the long-term plan that one has created. It is important to improve one's financial status knowing that mishaps will occur along the way. How to choose the path that will lead to one's financial success will differ from person to person. Hence, one should consider what one's financial value is and make short- and long-term plans and goals involving proper budgeting, staying away from future debt, and producing and saving money. As was mentioned earlier in the book, one should not buy expensive goods, but purchase what one needs and live within one's means. In doing so, the idea is to spend less than one earns so that one can participate in investment and retirement options. One should educate oneself about good and bad investments, partake in diverse investments, and make use of compound interest. If one is faithful, patient, and disciplined in frugal habits, the possibility of passing this way of life down through the generations is greater.

Money specialists explain that short-term in terms of cash should emphasize saving instead of investments. LaPonsie (2019) warns that folks make errors in terms of investments in the short run, being tempted by attractive interest rates, not comprehending that the yields typically involve risk and that the investment is unwise if they are likely to need the cash soon.

Comprehending one's own present finances and enhancing one's financial knowledge can aid in developing a financial plan and strategy to meet one's objectives (Friedberg, 2021c). In Chapter 4, the idea of savings and compound interest was emphasized which would differ depending on one's experience and actual savings. Nonetheless, the more one saves and builds on what one has, the more assets one may acquire, providing one with the potential to expand one's assets. Comprehending the marvel of compounding assets while simultaneously not making impulsive but keen choices will help increase one's savings and investments. As one's savings prosper, one can continue to educate oneself in terms of the market. Better comprehension of the market will provide more confidence and cautious selections in terms of the quantity of assets one wants to remain liquid (simply changed to cash) and what one wants to include in one's portfolio (Friedberg, 2021c).

Cash that one must have available should not be invested in the stock market, and cash that one is saving for the future (retirement) should not be placed in a simple savings account (O'Shea, 2021). A good short-term investment has solidity, liquidity, and low or no business charges. In addition, one should establish investment objectives, keep in mind risk and security, and focus on short-term investments centered on one's needs within the objectives (Royal, 2021b).

Dematteo (2020) quotes Bridget Todd of The Financial Gym as saying that one should focus on one's objectives and the period in which these objectives are to be met. Royal (2021b) explains that short-term securities are made up to about three years and for this short period, one will be confined to safe investments, staying away from more risky investments like stocks and stock funds. Dematteo continues to say that there is an abundance of investments to choose from, keeping in mind that the growth of low-risk investments is less but more predictable.

Royal (2021b) also suggests the idea of making short-term investments, using savings accounts, United States government and corporate bond funds, money market and cash management accounts, treasury certificates of deposit, and money market mutual funds. High risk investments have the possibility of fast growth but include more potential risk as the market fluctuates, causing one to lose cash. Therefore, one's short- and long-term objectives should involve a diverse investment portfolio with low and high risk.

If one is seeking an extended period of investing (over three years), keep in mind that the more extended the time, the better off one is. Securities like stocks are ideal due to greater potential on the return as the stock market has gone up 10%

yearly on a regular unstable basis over an extended time. An extended time helps the investor to deal with the fluctuation of the market (Royal, 2021b). If one's place of employment provides a 401(k), IRA, or a combination, one should realize that these are considered the mainstream of extended investment for retirement. These retirement investments are a plus and have tax benefits. Long-term investments should make use of a certain portion of stock securities if the duration is a decade or more since one has more latent time to deal with market fluctuations (O'Shea, 2021).

LaPonsie (2019) says that when looking at the long term, one should consider placing some portion of one's investments into stock market securities. For the most part, bear markets endure for 9 to 16 months, and one who invests for a five-year period can manage to risk an unstable short period in the market. One must consider that in order to play it carefully, one should start transferring cash to such investments as bonds and fixed income funds when the time is near to use these assets. Employees have to calculate how long they have to make good any losses before retirement, and they should transfer their cash to more cautious and minor risk securities as their professional career comes to an end (LaPonsie, 2019).

Friedberg (2021) believes that that people can easily obtain financial knowledge and expertise. Financial literacy touches each facet of one's life, including the amount one spends on food and where one lives. Good monetary and financial information enables one to make proper and astute investment decisions that can have a profound direct impact on one's future. You need to provide for yourself first and make financial arrangements with your cash so that each cent is in your favor and every penny works for you.

Short and Long Financial Tips from 'Big Al'

Alison Boord White, Provost and Vice President of Academic Affairs shared the following.

> I do not pretend to be any kind of financial wizard. My knowledge of finances is limited at best, and anything that I learned in graduate finance classes is mostly forgotten. I DO remember Time/Value/Money, but that's about it! And the old adage "Time is money" is true in so many respects.

MONEY HAS NO COMPLEXION

But honestly, that's about the extent of my financial wisdom. I DO have a few very basic tips that have worked well for me and my family over the years. We are not rich by any means, but with retirement around the corner, we have worked hard to build a nest egg. Basically, my philosophy is that little scraps here and there DO add up! So here goes.

When you get your first full-time job with benefits, and it has a retirement plan of any type, utilize it to its fullest. I was 23 when I landed my first full-time job with benefits. They had a matching program – the company matched the percentage of each paycheck that you set aside to go directly to that retirement plan. At the time, I believe the retirement percentage was 2% to 4% of your salary.

First, take out the maximum amount possible – there's usually a range, such as 2% to 4%. Go with the 4%, if at all possible. If you are making $1000 per paycheck, 4% is just $40! You won't even miss it if you never see it. (Most companies take it out before you get your actual paycheck – net pay.) That money will add up over the years, and you will need it down the road. If you had it now, it would likely be wasted on lunches or coffee. I was fortunate to have that matching plan, so that $40 immediately became $80 with the company's matching contribution. I'd made 100% on my investment already!

When you get that first credit card, DON'T go crazy. It's so easy these days to track your spending. Sign up to track your credit card expenditures online. You can check it as often as you want or need to, 24/7. Set a limit in your head to what you can afford each month, and don't go past it.

PAY OFF THAT CREDIT CARD BILL IN FULL EACH MONTH. DO NOT make minimum payments – credit card interest is insane at 18% plus, and then it compounds! If you pay the minimum amount for any period of time, you will end up paying for what you purchase two, three, or even four times! It is truly an unethical business that sucks many in. Don't be fooled. Use it for the convenience, but ALWAYS pay that credit card off FULLY!!

BY SCOTT GLENN

Keep a change jar. When it's full, cash it in and spend it on something fun, if you want. Go to dinner on it! This can be your "mad money!"

DO NOT buy coffee at Dunkin' Donuts every day. Do not eat lunch out every day. Treat yourself once or twice a week. It's not much money per day, but when you spend it 4 or 5 days a week, you are spending a large chunk of money. Think of coffee at $3/day for 5 days a week, 50 weeks a year – that adds up to $750 over the course of a year. What could you do with an extra $750?

Cars – we drove used cars for years and for years after the car was fully paid for. A monthly car payment that never ends can be a real drain on your finances. That said, all cars are expensive right now – so it's not a great time to buy a car – used or new! Shop carefully if you must buy one now. Car availability is low currently, so the prices are zooming up! (Scarcity is not the consumer's friend; it tips supply/demand in the seller's favor!)

STEER CLEAR OF PURSPURINSTANT PURCHASING FOR INSTANT GRATIFICATION!! It's okay to splurge and buy yourself a candy bar, or a smoothie, on occasion. However, DO NOT buy expensive items on an impulse – things like cars, homes, or even appliances. Sometimes we get tired of that old refrigerator, and a nice, new energy-efficient stainless steel bottom freezer model would be so awesome in the kitchen!!! But the old one is working just fine, and the saving from energy efficiency, although it looks good, is probably negligible over a year's time. (It would never pay you back for the purchase or do anything even close! We are probably talking less than $100 a year!) If it works, keep it. Save up for that new, shiny refrigerator and watch for sales. Then the purchase will be much easier on your pocketbook!

Set yourself a limit that you can afford for impulse purchases – something pretty low that fits in your budget – say $50 – anything I buy over $50 will be accounted for and planned in my budgeting. I will start saving for it, and I will look for sales to keep the price of a large purchase as reasonable as possible!

MONEY HAS NO COMPLEXION

When you purchase a home, try to establish equity in your home as quickly as possible. Make paying that mortgage a priority, and if you can pay it off early, do so. It will save you money! You can also use it to get low interest home equity loans or line of credit. We used our Home Equity Line of Credit to pay off our children's school loans. It was 3% interest instead of 8%! That is a substantial savings.

Any time, you have a loan or mortgage, even a car loan, try to pay a little extra toward the principal each month to pay it off early. Every little bit helps! You'll be amazed how much it will save you down the road. Even if you have a low interest rate, interest accrues over time.

Get your credit rating established early, and make sure that it's good! 850 is the maximum. If you can get your credit score over 800, you can qualify for the lowest interest rate when purchasing big ticket items such as a car.

If you can manage a small amount to save on your own in addition to whatever retirement plan you are contributing to at work, do so. Again, it may not be much. But if you can transfer just $25 to a savings account, to start, each month from your paycheck, it does two things. It allows you to build a little rainy-day fund. Second, you are not entirely dependent upon that retirement plan – not all of your proverbial eggs are in one basket! Diversity is ALWAYS important when saving.

Always have both a savings and a checking account, and consciously transfer some money from checking to savings each month to save for items you want to buy and save for big bills that come up periodically, such as insurance and taxes.

As soon as you get that savings account to a reasonable amount, take half of it and find a financial planner whom you trust implicitly. Not all financial planners are created equal!! I find that word of mouth reputation may be the best. You could start with as little as a couple of hundred dollars. A truly good financial planner will recognize and appreciate your interest in getting started and will advise you well.

Anyone "not interested" in just a couple of hundred dollars who just wants high dollar clients is not the person you want managing your money anyway! I was fortunate to know someone through work who taught finance and then became a financial planner. I knew he was as honest, and he was a wonderful help to me and my husband through the years.

Keep your checkbook balanced!!! If you have regular transfers or bills that are paid, be sure you always have that information available.

Use spreadsheets such as Excel to help you set up your budget and keep track of expenditures. Keep it current. This enables you to set up your finances in ways that you understand.

COUPONS – are great! They save you money, right? Not always!!! If you buy something you normally wouldn't buy and then don't use it, you spent money that you wouldn't have otherwise for no gain. If you buy more than you normally would, you are spending more money overall upfront. Be sure if you use a coupon, that you buy something you will use and not waste.

In short, there are lots of little things you do that can add up and save you money. You can then invest that money!!

MONEY HAS NO COMPLEXION

CHAPTER 12

AFTERWORD

The historical effects of the wealth and income gap on marginalized people of color, in particular Blacks, continue to this day. Although this book is targeted at marginalized people of color, some of the input and experiences are from nonmarginalized people (Whites) which emphasizes and has been proven through history that all walks of life are needed to create change. The general systems theory and interactive social system reinforce this by explaining that we were not meant to be alone and that changing and redeveloping laws and society is imperative. So, voting is important, and we all must work out our differences and emphasize what we have in common. The past of marginalized people of color has much negativity, but a confident attitude will aid the process of transformation into positive action that is contagious. In doing so, one has a better chance to be successful in one's financial decisions and in a frugal lifestyle that can lead to appropriate and knowledgeable investments.

No money can buy happiness, but it does help in making a living. One can still have an enjoyable life without overspending or trying to "keep up with the Joneses." Sound discipline and acquiring valuable knowledge will help to balance out income, savings, and expenses, which involves a trade-off (opportunity cost) in our daily financial decision-making process. What one does today has a profound effect on tomorrow. Therefore, simplicity, knowledge, and frugality will help people to make investments in securities such as stocks, bonds, mutual funds, ETFs, and others, as explained in detail in this book. Knowledge is powerful. Keep in mind that if available, proper use of a 401(k), 503(b), and Roth IRA are amazing investments in terms of employment and investing in property is as well.

Real estate investments are somewhat an investing secret, especially with the use of REIT. One should research and examine this type of investment to make sure it is suitable in one's planning. If not, there are various alternative investment ideas such as the hot cryptocurrency fusion, website flipping, and various commodity investments. One should keep in mind that no matter what investments one indulges in, one must diversify one's portfolio or choices. Every investor should have a simple knowledge and understanding of how business and entrepreneurship operate, what they involve, and what makes them successful. This knowledge will provide insight into what a company is about and aid one's decisions just as the various financial forms give the numeric and expressive position of the entity.

Michael Blackson, Associate Vice President of Surveillance at Nasdaq says,

> I have worked for over 13 years with Nasdaq and 15 years with the Philadelphia Stock Exchange before it was acquired by Nasdaq. My primary role and responsibilities are to surveil and regulate Nasdaq PHLX (Philadelphia Stock Exchange) options trading floor in Philadelphia, Pennsylvania. Nasdaq PHLX is one of six physical options trading floors in the United States. I also surveil and regulate Nasdaq's six fully electronic options exchanges: Nasdaq PHLX, Nasdaq Options Market (NOM), Nasdaq BX Options Market, Nasdaq ISE (International Stock Exchange), Nasdaq GEMX (Gemini), and Nasdaq MRX (Mercury).

> Nasdaq is a self-regulatory organization and was the world's first fully electronic stock exchange established in February 1971. Nasdaq was initially an acronym for the National Association of Securities Dealers Automated Quotations. The creation of Nasdaq was from the National Association of Securities Dealers (NASD), now known as the Financial Industry Regulation Authority (FINRA). Originally, NASD licensed brokerage firms and individual broker-dealers regulated the firm account and trading activity. Over the years, Nasdaq decided to become more than just a stock exchange and envisioned the company as a full-service organization for listed stocks and brokerage firms providing services, such as product support, marketing, technology, and surveillance services. Nasdaq is now a global organization as it

MONEY HAS NO COMPLEXION

acquired eight Nordic stock exchanges through the acquisition of the OMX. Through many Nasdaq acquisitions, it became one of the largest exchange operators in the world, offering an array of products and services for brokerage firms and other financial institutions.

By acquiring the Philadelphia Stock Exchange, Nasdaq became part owner of the Options Clearing Corporation (OCC). The OCC was established in 1973 by the Chicago Board of Options Exchange (CBOE). The CBOE was the first options exchange established in 1973. As options trading began to grow, the OCC and the options exchanges knew there was only a sector of brokerage firms that fully understood the financial vehicle of options trading. There was no primary source of education on options trading, so the CBOE and the OCC created the Options Institute. The OCC's primary purpose was to provide clearing and settlement services for options trading for all United States options exchanges and brokerage clearing firms such as Bank of America and Goldman Sachs. The Options Institute's primary purpose is to educate the retail and broker-dealer industry about options trading and how it is used as a hedging product to protect investor stock portfolios. The OCC has become the world's largest clearing corporation for option products and the primary source of education and understanding of the risk, strategies, and benefits of options trading.

Financial literacy was not part of my childhood education at home or school when I was growing up in the heart of West Philadelphia, raised by my great-grandparents. My parents only taught me to be a hard worker, pay bills, and make enough money to provide for my family. They did not teach me how to manage my money or how to establish good credit. After graduating from high school, I enrolled at Jefferson Business School and earned a certificate in computer-processing, but I still did not learn about saving, investing, and finances. After graduating from business school in March 1989, I applied for the data entry operator position at the Philadelphia Stock Exchange. As a data entry operator, I worked on the options trading floor to assist the traders with data entry of its quotes and trades.

After 10 months as a data entry operator, I started my career in surveillance and market regulation with the Philadelphia Stock Exchange in January 1990. I had no formal undergraduate degree and did not understand the purpose of market surveillance and market regulation. The Philadelphia Stock Exchange gave me the opportunity based on my willingness to learn and adapt. I am sure affirmative action played a role in my advancement, but the little-known fact is that I applied for the market surveillance secretary position because I could type 100 words a minute. Sad to say, I typed only 60 words a minute on the typing test, but the head of the department offered me the market surveillance analyst position. I was the youngest and first African American given this position in the market surveillance department. I quickly advanced from analyst to manager of the trading floor in the matter of 4 years with no formal degree. That upset my non-African American colleagues in the department. Affirmative action may have got my foot in the door, but my career would not be where it is today without me applying myself and demonstrating the skills necessary to advance further within the department and ultimately in the company.

As I learned more about trading, I still knew very little about investments and finances as my career in surveillance and market regulation excelled faster than my understanding of the financial industry itself. It took about 10 years of my career to fully understand the importance of saving and investing in my financial future. From my experience, the lack of financial education in the school system curriculum and not having a support system in the home is why the Black community is underrepresented in the investor community.

While working on the PHLX options trading floor, I was fortunate to meet only two African American traders out of 300 traders who worked on the trading floor. These individuals were Warren West and Reginald Browne, who became the most successful and influential traders in the stock market industry. Mr. West and Mr. Browne were the role models who taught me the value of financial education and that we are our only obstacles regardless of the opposition.

MONEY HAS NO COMPLEXION

As the future of African Americans in the financial community continues to grow, private charter schools and nonprofit organizations are providing financial literacy courses to the younger generation. The majority of my generation did not receive the proper guidance and education in the early part of our lives to establish an impactful foundational knowledge. The future generation of entrepreneurs, investors, and business owners will know at an early stage that will ultimately place them at the forefront of the financial and investment industry. Throughout my career, I had the opportunity to visit high schools and colleges to speak to students about trading, investing, and finances. These students believed that trading or investing required a large amount of money to begin trading and investing. Anyone 18 years or older can start a brokerage account and start investing or trading with no more than $100.00. Mutual funds are the best option for anyone looking for long-term growth. Also, anyone looking to start investing or trading should educate themselves by finding the proper resources to understand the risks and rewards of trading and investments.

As retail investors embrace cryptocurrency, they would like municipal governments to make this new currency acceptable for goods and services. Cryptocurrencies are listed on Nasdaq and New York Stock Exchange and are available for trading. The value of cryptocurrency has increased tremendously over the years, and investors believe municipal governments will soon accept it. I cannot speak about Nasdaq and how the organization plans to adopt this new wave of cryptocurrencies, such as Bitcoin and Dogecoin. The financial community believes that cryptocurrency will be the future of money as many investors are moving away from physical forms of currency. All investments have their inherited risks and rewards, but that should not stop anyone from taking the opportunity to start learning, earning, and growing a financial future.

Educating the youth of our country in the areas of financial planning and generational wealth is just as valuable as any other type of education. We must teach the next generation of African Americans about the value of money, saving, and investing. The more we teach our young adults about their financial future, the more represented our people will be in this new era of trading, investing, and financial wealth.

Whether one invest in financial facets or not, one should consider investing in appropriate true love as one can see the positive effects through the cited scripture and input of a few contributors within this book. TRUE Love ALWAYS has a positive return on investment (long and short term), and the more love is accepted, the more LOVE compounds with great multiplication causing a contagious effect to all who accept! Most imperative, LOVE has been paid in full!

Blessings to all and health and well-being in life! Stay positive in faith with motivation and appropriate love, no matter what!

Dr. Scott Glenn

REFERENCES

Alcorn, C. (2021). *Black-owned banks are booming, and they're pouring money back into their communities.* CCN. https://amp-cnn-com.cdn.ampproject.org/c/s/amp.cnn.com/cnn/2021/06/09/economy/black-owned-banks/index.html

Amadeo, K. (2020). *Racial wealth gap in the United States.* The Balance. https://www.thebalance.com/racial-wealth-gap-in-united-states-4169678

Amadeo, K. (2021). *Home equity and the racial wealth gap.* The Balance. https://www.thebalance.com/how-home-equity-drives-the-racial-wealth-gap-4178236

Annie E. Casey Foundation. (2016). *Investing in tomorrow: Helping families build savings and assets* [Online policy brief]. https://www.aecf.org/resources/investing-in-tomorrow-helping-families-build-savings-and-assets

Asante-Muhammad, D., Collins, C., Hoxie, J., & Nieves, E. (2017). *The road to zero wealth. How the racial wealth divide is hollowing out America's middle class.* https://prosperitynow.org/files/PDFs/road_to_zero_wealth.pdf

Ask Money. (2020). *What are ETF investments?* Retrieved August 20, 2020, from https://www.askmoney.com/investing/what-are-etf-investments

Assari, S. (2018). Health disparities due to diminished return among Black Americans. *Social Issues and Policy Review, 2*(1), 112–45. Retrieved December 12, 2021 from EBSCOhost

Becker, G., & Murphy, K. M. (2007). *The upside of income inequality.* American Enterprise Institute. https://www.aei.org/articles/the-upside-of-income-inequality/

Bell, A.M., Chetty, R., Jaravel, X., Petkova, N., & van Reenen, J. (2017). *Who becomes an inventor in America? The importance of exposure to innovation* (Working Paper 24062). National Bureau of Economic Research. https://www. nber.org/papers/w24062

Berry, J. (2007). The origins of the human capital concept. *The Cutter Edge.* Cutter Consortium.. Retrieved January 5, 2014, from http://www.cutter.com

Bertocchi, G., & Dimico, A. (2010, November 14). *The historical roots of inequality.* VoxEU. https://voxeu.org/article/historical-roots-inequality-evidence-slavery-us

Bovaird, C. (2020, July 8). *Corporate bonds: Advantages and disadvantages.* Investopedia. Retrieved August 19, 2021, from https://www.investopedia.com/articles/investing/080916/corporate-bonds-advantages-and-disadvantages.asp

Carlozo, L. (2012). Black Americans donate to make a difference. Retrieved December 25, 2021 from Black Americans donate to make a difference | Reuters

Carnevale, A. P., Rose, S. J., & Cheah, B. (n.d.). *The college payoff: Education, occupations, lifetime earnings.* Georgetown University, Center on Education and the Workforce. https://www2.ed.gov/policy/highered/reg/hearulemaking/2011/collegepayoff.pdf

Chen. J. (2021a). *Growth and income fund.* Investopedia. Retrieved August 17, 2021, from https://www.investopedia.com/terms/g/growth-income-fund.asp

Chen, J. (2021b). *Real estate investment trust (REIT).* Investopedia. Retrieved August 18, 2021, from https://www.investopedia.com/terms/r/reit.asp

Cheng, M. (2021). *401(k) and 403(b) Plans: Knowing the difference.* Investopedia. Retrieved August 18, 2021, from https://www.investopedia.com/ask/answers/100314/what-difference-between-401k-plan-and-403b-plan.asp

Choe, S. (2020). Stocks are soaring, and most Black people are missing out. Retrieved December 29, 2021 from https://abcnews.go.com/Business/wireStory/stocks-soaring-black-people-missing-73567655

Chron Contributor. (May 17, 2021). *Why is it important to entrepreneurs to develop financial plans for their companies?* https://smallbusiness.chron.com/important-entrepreneurs-develop-financial-plans-companies-73993.html

Clement, D. (2018, July 31). *The wealth gap and the race between stocks and homes.* Retrieved May 11, 2021, from https://www.minneapolisfed.org/article/2018/the-wealth-gap-and-the-race-between-stocks-and-homes

Coates, T-N. (2014, June). The case for reparations. *The Atlantic.* https://www.theatlantic.com/magazine/archive/2014/06/the-case-for-reparations/361631/

Darity, W., Jr. (2019). *A new agenda for eliminating racial inequality in the United States: The research we need.* William T. Grant Foundation. http://wtgrantfoundation.org/library/uploads/2019/01/A-New-Agenda-for-Eliminating-Racial-Inequality-in-the-United-States_WTG-Digest-2018

Darity, W., Jr., Hamilton, D., Paul, M., Aja, A., Price, A., Moore, A., & Chiopris, C. (2018). *What we get wrong about closing the racial wealth gap.* Samuel DuBois Cook Center on Social Equity. Insight Center for Community Economic Development. https://socialequity.duke.edu/wp-content/uploads/2019/10/what-we-get-wrong.pdf

Davis, G. B. (2021). *Pros & cons of investing with robo-advisors – Are they for you?* Retrieved August 22, 2021, from https://www.moneycrashers.com/pros-cons-investing-robo-advisors/

Dematteo, M. (2020). *There's 'a lot of life to live' before age 59: How to invest your savings for both short- and long-term goals.* Retrieved August 22, 2021, from https://www.cnbc.com/select/how-to-invest-savings-short-long-term-goals/

Devani, N. (2019, April 14). *What "financials" mean for early-stage start-ups.* Medium. https://medium.com/@neildevani/what-financials-means-for-early-stage-startups-a-guide-for-founders-33af6ae7d274

DeWitt, L. (2010). The decision to exclude agricultural and domestic workers from the 1935 Social Security Act. *Social Security Bulletin, 70*(4), 49–68. Retrieved December 3, 2021 from EBSCOhost.

Dorson, K. (2020, February 4). *Market and investment evaluation methods.* Retrieved September 1, 2020, from https://www.wiseworldinvestment.com/blog/market-and-investment-evaluation-methods

Dummies. (n.d.). *Risks with Investing in Commodities.* https://www.dummies.com/personal-finance/investing/risks-with-investing-in-commodities/

Dunn, (n.d.). Make compound magic work for you - PERSONAL INVESTMENT. *Australian, The.* Psychological Association.

Edwards, J. (2020, July 5). *The pros and cons of indexes.* Investopedia. Retrieved August 12, 2021, from https://www.investopedia.com/articles/investing/011316/pros-and-cons-indexes.asp

Fidelity Learning Center. (2021). *What is commodity investing?* Retrieved August 24, 2021, from https://www.fidelity.com/learning-center/investment-products/mutual-funds/about-commodity-investing

Four kinds of crowdfunding: Loans, donations, exchanges, and equity. (n.d.) Retrieved October 5, 2021, from http://www.toolsforbusiness.info/success/crowdfunding_kinds.pdf

Frankenfield, J. (2021). *Cryptocurrency.* Investopedia. Retrieved August 21, 2921, from https://www.investopedia.com/terms/c/cryptocurrency.asp

Friedberg, B. (Ed.). (2015). *Personal finance: An encyclopedia of modern money management.* Greenwood.

Friedberg, B. (2021a). *Achieve simple financial success with 5 good financial habits.* Retrieved August 22, 2021, from https://barbarafriedbergpersonalfinance.com/5-personal-finance-habits-to-help-you-achieve-financial-freedom/

Friedberg, B. (2021b). *Best robo-advisors – 2021.* Retrieved August 6, 2021, from https://www.roboadvisorpros.com/best-robo-advisors/

Friedberg, B. (2021c). *The financial planning process – Steps to wealth.* Retrieved August 16, 2021, from https://barbarafriedbergpersonalfinance.com/financial-planning-process/

Friedberg, B. (2021d). *Pros and cons of REITs – Should I invest?* Retrieved August 16, 2021, from https://barbarafriedbergpersonalfinance.com/should-invest-real-estate-now-quick-easy-ways-invest-real-estatepart/

Friedberg, B. A. (2021e, October 7). *Pros & cons of using a robo-advisor.* Investopedia. Retrieved August 22, 2021, from https://www.investopedia.com/articles/personal-finance/010616/pros-cons-using-roboadvisor.asp

Galli, S. and Ronnback, K. (2021). Land distribution and inequality in a black settler colony: the case of Sierra Leone, Economic History Review, 74, 1 (2021), pp. 115–1371792. Retrieved December 24, 2021 from Land distribution and inequality in a black settler colony: the case of Sierra Leone, 1792–1831† - Galli - 2021 - The Economic History Review - Wiley Online Library

Glassman, J. K. (2021). The Truth About Index Funds. *Kiplinger's Personal Finance, 75*(10), 31–32. Retrieved December 10, 2021 from EBSCOhost

Glenn, S. (2016). *Teaching in Higher Ed. A Plan of Action.* Published by DIVERSITY in Ed Magazine Spring 2016. Retrieved June 12, 2021 from https://www.diversityined.com/magazine

Glenn, S. (2010). *A qualitative ethnographic study of african american leadership in higher education administration* (Order No. 3405504). Available from Dissertations & Theses @ University of Phoenix. (193939445). https://www.proquest.com/dissertations-theses/qualitative-ethnographic-study-african-american/docview/193939445/se-2?accountid=35812

K. L., Glick, D. M., & Palmer, M. (2020). Neighborhood Defenders: Participatory Politics and America's Housing Crisis. *Political Science Quarterly (Wiley-Blackwell), 135*(2), 281–312. https://doi.org/10.1002/polq.13035

Goldin, C. (2002). What produced the human capital century? *New England Economic Review,* 00284726. Business Source Complete. Retrieved December 12, 2021 from EBSCOhost.

Gotanda, H., Jha, A. K., Li, K. T., Kominski, G. F., & Tsugawa, Y. (2020). Out-of-pocket spending and financial burden among low-income adults after Medicaid expansions in the United States: Quasi-experimental difference-in-difference study. *The British Medical Journal, 398.* https://doi.org/10.1136/bmj.m40

Graves-Fitzsimmons, G., & Siddiqi, M. (2021, May 7). *Faith leaders highlight how the American Jobs Plan invests in U.S. communities.* Center for American Progress. https://americanprogress.org/article/faith-leaders-highlight-american-jobs-plan-invests-u-s-communities

Green, W. (2021). *Richer, wiser, happier: How the world's greatest investors win in markets and life.* Scribner.

Gumnior, E. C., Richards, E.L. (1992). Revealing, Addressing, and Redressing Ethnocentricity: Teaching International Business Law with Process Response Journals. Retrieved December 26, 2021 from ERIC - ED347912 - Revealing, Addressing, and Redressing Ethnocentricity: Teaching International Business Law with Process Response Journals., 1992-Mar-26

Hagler, J. (2015, May 28). *8 facts you should know about the criminal justice system and people of color.* Center for American Progress. https://www.americanprogress.org/issues/race/news/2015/05/28/113436/8-facts-you-should-know-about-the-criminaljustice-system-and-people-of-color/

Hanks, A., Solomon, D., & Weller, C. (2018, February 21). *Systematic inequality: How America's structural racism helped create the Black-White wealth gap.* Center for American Progress. https://www.americanprogress.org/article/systematic-inequality/

Hayes, A. (2021, August 31). *Rebound.* Investopedia. Retrieved September 20, 2021, from https://www.investopedia.com/articles/personal-finance/010616/pros-cons-using-roboadvisor.asp

Hicks, C. (2020, September 29). How to recover after loss in the stock market. *U.S. News.* https://money.usnews.com/investing/investing-101/articles/how-to-recover-after-loss-in-the-stock-market

Inequality.org. (2021). *The facts that define our grand divides.* https://inequality.org/facts/

Jain, A. (2021, March 11). These are the top 10 crowdfunding platforms. *Entrepreneur United States.* https://www.entrepreneur.com/article/366972

Johnson, G. A. (2020, September 2). *How do Black people spend their money? The racial wealth gap.* Black Men in America. https://blackmeninamerica.com/updated-how-do-black-people-spend-their-money-3/

Jones, C. P. (2000). Levels of racism: A theoretic framework and a gardener's tale. *American Journal of Public Health, 90* (8), 1212–15. Retrieved December 5, 2021 from EBSCOhost

Jones, J. (2017, February 12). *The racial wealth gap. How African Americans have been shortchanged out of the materials to build wealth.* Economic Policy Institute. Retrieved May 10, 2021, from https://www.epi.org/blog/the-racial-wealth-gap-how-african-americans-have-been-shortchanged-out-of-the-materials-to-build-wealth/

Kennon, J. (2021, July 29). *What is the difference between stocks and index funds?* The Balance. Retrieved August 20, 2021, from https://www.thebalance.com/stocks-vs-index-funds-which-is-right-for-your-portfolio-358083

Kijakazi, K., Brown, S., Charleston, D., & Runes, C. (2019, May 23). *Next50 catalyst brief: Structural racism.* Urban Institute. https://www.urban.org/research/publication/next50-catalyst-brief-structural-racism

Kijakazi, K., Smith, K., & Runes, C. (2019, July). *African American economic security and the role of social security.* Urban Institute. https://www.urban.org/sites/default/files/publication/100697/african_american_economic_security_and_the_role_of_social_security.pdf

Kiker, B. F. (1966). The historical roots of human capital. *Journal of Political Economy, 74*(5), 481–499. https://doi.org/10.1086/259201

Kowalski, C. (2021). *Should your investment portfolio include commodities?* Retrieved August 24, 2021, from https://www.thebalance.com/how-much-commodities-investment-809211

LaPonsie, M. (2019, September 26). How to invest for the short and long term. *US News*. https://money.usnews.com/investing/investing-101/articles/how-to-invest-your-money-for-the-short-and-long-term

Lee, A. G. (2021, May 12). *The history of cryptocurrency: Bitcoin's long, strange trip to best-performing asset of the decade*. Esquire. Retrieved August 22, 2021 from https://www.esquire.com/lifestyle/money/g36290032/history-of-cryptocurrency/

Little, K. (2021, August 30). *What is cryptocurrency?* Retrieved August 22, 2021 from https://time.com/nextadvisor/investing/cryptocurrency/what-is-cryptocurrency/

Littauer, S. L. (1994). Keys to successful stock investing. *Consumers' Research Magazine, 77*(9), 26. Retrieved December 12, 2021 from EBSCOhost

Locke, T. (2021, May 3). *3 investing lessons Warren Buffett shared at the 2021 Berkshire Hathaway meeting*. CNBC. https://www.cnbc.com/2021/05/03/investing-lessons-from-warren-buffett-at-berkshire-hathaway-meeting.html

Maffatt, M. (2019, September 12). *What is a commodity in economics?* https://www.thoughtco.com/commodity-economics-definition-1146936

McIntosh, K., Moss, E., Nunn, R., & Shambaugh, J. (2020, February 27). *Examining the Black-White wealth gap*. The Brookings Institute. https://www.brookings.edu/blog/up-front/2020/02/27/examining-the-black-white-wealth-gap/

Mitchell, C. (2021). *Bouncing back after a big trading loss*. The Balance. Retrieved September 21, 2021, from https://www.thebalance.com/bouncing-back-after-a-big-trading-loss-4005884

M1 Finance. (2021). *My gains and losses*. Retrieved September 21, 2021, from https://support.m1finance.com/hc/en-us/articles/115015329187-My-gains-and-losses

Muhammad, D. A., Tec, R., & Ramirez, K. (2019, November 18). *Racial wealth snapshot: American Indians/Native Americans*. National Community

Reinvestment Coalition. https://ncrc.org/racial-wealth-snapshot-american-indians-native-americans/

Napoletano, E., & Curry, B. (2021). *Fixed-income basics: What is a bond?* Forbes Advisor. Retrieved August 18, 2021, from https://www.forbes.com/advisor/investing/what-is-a-bond/

Nareit. (2021). *History of REITs and real estate investing.* Retrieved August 18, 2021, from https://www.reit.com/what-reit/history

National Debt Relief. (2016). *Frugal living starts with your definition of wants and needs.* Retrieved August 4, 2021, from https://www.nationaldebtrelief.com/frugal-living-starts-definition-wants-needs/

National Philanthropic Trust. (2016). *A history of modern philanthropy.* Retrieved June 25, 2021, from https://www.historyofgiving.org/

Nellis, A. (2016). *The color of justice: Racial and ethnic disparity in state prisons.* The Sentencing Project. https://www.sentencingproject.org/publications/color-of-justice-racial-and-ethnic-disparity-in-state-prisons/

Nielson, (2015). Black Influence Goes Mainstream in the U.S. Retrieved from Black Influence Goes Mainstream in the U.S. – Nielsen

Nunn, N. (2007, December 8). *The historical origins of Africa's underdevelopment.* VoxEU. https://voxeu.org/article/slave-trade-and-african-underdevelopment

O'Shea, A. (2021, April 15). *How to invest your savings for short-term or long-term goals.* Retrieved September 3, 2021, from https://www.nerdwallet.com/article/investing/invest-savings-short-intermediate-long-term-goals

Palmer, B. (2021). *Mutual funds: Advantages and disadvantages.* Investopedia. Retrieved August 20, 2021 from https://www.investopedia.com/ask/answers/10/mutual-funds-advantages-disadvantages.asp

Pant, P. (2021, June 22). *What are the S&P 500, Nasdaq, and the Dow?* The Balance. Retrieved August 18, 2021, from https://www.thebalance.com/the-sandp-500-nasdaq-dow-jones-what-is-this-stuff-453745

Pat S. (2011, October 10). *What are municipal bonds – pros & cons of investing.* Retrieved August 14, 2021 from https://www.moneycrashers.com/municipal-bonds-investing/.

Perea, J. F. (2014). Doctrines of delusion: How the history of the G.I. Bill and other inconvenient truths undermine the Supreme Court's affirmative action jurisprudence. *University of Pittsburgh Law Review, 75*(4), 583. https://doi.org/10.5195/lawreview.2014.344

Perrius, C. (2011).Targeted Universalism. Creating a World that Works for All of Us. Retrieved December 25, 2021 from Targeted Universalism | infinite hope | the national equity project blog archive

Perry, A. M. and Romer, C. (2020). To expand the economy, invest in black businesses. Retrieved December 24, 2021 from https://www.brookings.edu/

Pew Charitable Trusts. (2010). *Collateral costs: Incarceration's effect on economic mobility.* https://www.pewtrusts.org/~/media/legacy/uploadedfiles/pcs_assets/2010/collateralcosts1pdf

Phillips J. (2005). The value of human capital: What logic and intuition tell us. *Chief Learning Officer, 4*(8), 50-52. Available from: Business Source Complete, Ipswich, MA.

Poole, M. (2006). *The segregated origins of social security: African Americans and the welfare state.* University of North Carolina Press. Retrieved December 11, 2021 from EBSCOhost

Posell, J. (n.d.). *Start-ups & financial models and plans: Why they are important.* Fullstack Finance. https://fullstackfinance.com/startups-financial-modelsplans-why-they-are-important/

Pound, J. (2021, May 1). *This is the special lesson Warren Buffett gave new stock investors at his annual meeting.* CNBC. https://www.cnbc.com/2021/05/01/this-is-the-special-lesson-warren-buffett-gave-new-stock-investors-at-his-annual-meeting.html

Powell, J.A., Menendian, S., & Ake, W. (2019). *Targeted universalism: Policy and practice*. Haas Institute. https://belonging.berkeley.edu/sites/default/files/targeted_universalism_primer.pdf

Profile Tree. (n.d). *Website flipping: How to flip websites for profit*. Retrieved October 2, 2021, from https://profiletree.com/website-flipping/

Quadagno, J. (1988). *The transformation of old age security: Class and politics in the American welfare state*. University of Chicago Press.

Reece, R. L. (2020). The gender of colorism: Understanding the intersection of skin tone and gender inequality. *Journal of Economics, Race, and Policy, 4*, 47–55. https://doi.org/10.1007/s41996-020-00054-1

Reed, W. (2017, May 24). How Blacks' dollars can achieve Black power. *The Washington Informer*. https://www.washingtoninformer.com/business-exchange-how-blacks-dollars-can-achieve-black-power/

Retire Certain. (n.d.). How to evaluate an investment. Retrieved September 1, 2021, from https://retirecertain.com/how-to-evaluate-an-investment/

Roberge, E. (2019). *A financial planner explains when you should consider investing with a robo-adviser — and when you shouldn't*. Retrieved August 21, 2021 from https://www.businessinsider.com/personal-finance/pros-cons-robo-advisers-from-financial-planner

Rodley, J. (2021). *Website flipping: How to make money building, buying & selling sites*. Retrieved October 2, 2021, from https://jaserodley.com/website-flipping/

Rouse, C., Bernstein, J., Knudsen, H., and Zhang, J. (2021). Exclusionary Zoning: Its Effect on   Racial Discrimination in the Housing Market | .Retrieved December 24, 2021 from www.whitehouse.gov

Royal, J. (2021a). *How to invest in commodities*. Retrieved August 24, 2021, from https://www.bankrate.com/investing/how-to-invest-in-commodities/

Royal, J. (2021b). *8 best short-term investments in September 2021*. Retrieved September 3, 2021 from https://www.bankrate.com/investing/best-short-term-investments/

Royal, J. (2021c). *What is a bond ETF and is it a good investment?* Bankrate. Retrieved September 15, 2021, from https://www.bankrate.com/investing/bond-etfs-portfolio-benefits/amp/

Salam, R. (2012). The agenda. Brief thoughts on human capital investment. *National Review Online*. Retrieved October 3, 2013, from https://www.nationalreview.com/

Sankar-Bergmann, A., & Shorter, C. (2016, April 28). *Out of prison, but shackled in debt*. https://prosperitynow.org/blog/out-prison-shackled-debt

Sather, A. (2021, April 23). *10 reasons why compounding interest is the 8th wonder of the world*. Retrieved June 25, 2021, from https://einvestingforbeginners.com/compounding-interest/

Schermerhorn, C. (2019a). *Teaching America's racial wealth gap* [PowerPoint slides]. Arizona Council for History Education. https://calscherm.files.wordpress.com/09/2019/ache-racial-wealth-gap07-09-19-.pptx

Schermerhorn, C. (2019b). Why the racial wealth gap persists, more than 150 years after emancipation - The Washington Post. Retrieved November 1, 2021 from www.washingtonpost.com/outlook/2019/why-racial-wealth-gap-persists-more-than-years-after-emanciaption

Schrange, M. (2012). *Who do you want customers to become?* Harvard Business Review Press.

Schulz, N. (n.d.). *Human capital in a global age*. U.S. Chamber of Commerce Foundation. https://www.uschamberfoundation.org/bhq/human-capital-global-age

Schwab-Pomerantz, C. (2020, August 5). *Do asset allocation and diversification still work?* Retrieved September 20, 2021, from https://www.schwab.com/resource-center/insights/content/do-asset-allocation-and-diversification-still-work

Shapiro, T. M. (2004). *The hidden cost of being African American: How wealth perpetuates inequality.* Oxford University Press.

Sidner, S. (2016, October 4). *Tulsa shooting stirs memories of bloody race riot.* CNN. https://edition.cnn.com/2016/10/04/us/tulsa-race-riot-memories

Smart Asset. (2021, November). *7 secrets smart professionals use to choose financial advisors.* https://article.smartasset.com/financial-advisor-secrets-1/?utm_campaign=fli__falc_content_fasecrets&utm_term=flipboard_tech_nl_091521&utm_source=flipboard_nl&utm_content=ppl_ret_comf_trajectory_gary

Smedley, B. D. (2007). Why health care equity is essential. In B. D. Smedley & A. Jenkins (Eds.), *All things being equal.* The New Press in cooperation with Opportunity Agenda.

Stanfield, R., & Nicolaou, C. (2000). *Social security out of step with the modern family.* Urban Institute. Retrieved December 24, 2021 from Social Security: Out of Step with the Modern Family (urban.org)

Stoesz, D. (2016). *The excluded: An estimate of the consequences of denying social security to agricultural and domestic workers.* Washington University in St. Louis, Center for Social Development Research.

Sullivan, L., Meschede, T., Dietrich, L., Shapiro, T., Traub, A., Ruetschlin, C., & Draut, T. (2020). *The racial wealth gap: Why policy matters.* https://www.demos.org/sites/default/files/publications/RacialWealthGap_2.pdf

Thompson, J., & Weller C.E. (2016). *Wealth inequality among Asian Americans greater than among Whites.* Center for American Progress. https://www.americanprogress.org/article/wealth-inequality-among-asian-americans-greater-than-among-whites/

Tilbury, A. (2011). Turbocharged savings plan Make your money work Get on the compound interest bandwagon and your investment will accelerate from an amble to a sprint. *Townsville Bulletin*, 34.

Traub, A., Sullivan, L., Meschede, T, & Shapiro, T. (2017, February 6). *The asset value of whiteness: Understanding the racial wealth gap.* https://www.demos.org/research/asset-value-whiteness-understanding-racial-wealth-gap

Vinelli, A., & Weller, A. C. (2021). *The path to higher, more inclusive economic growth and good jobs.* Center for American Progress. https://www.americanprogress.org/article/path-higher-inclusive-economic-growth-good-jobs/

U.S. Bureau of Labor Statistics. (2021, October 19). *Median usual weekly earnings of full-time wage and salary workers by selected characteristics, quarterly averages, not seasonally adjusted* [Economic news release]. https://www.bls.gov/news.release/wkyeng.t02.htm

U.S. Census Bureau. (2015, May). *21.3 percent of U.S. population participates in government assistance programs each month* [Press release]. https://www.census.gov/newsroom/press-releases/2015/cb15-97.html.

U.S. Securities and Exchange Commission. (n.d). *Beginners' guide to asset allocation, diversification, and rebalancing.* Retrieved September 20, 2021 from https://www.investor.gov/additional-resources/general-resources/publications-research/info-sheets/beginners-guide-asset

Website Builders. (2020). *Website flipping: What is it and can anyone do it? The 2020 guide.* Retrieved October 2, 2021, from https://websitebuilders.com/how-to/case-studies/website-flipping/

Williams, T. R. (2003). *Asset-building policy as a response to wealth inequality: Drawing implications from the Homestead Act.* Washington University in St. Louis, Center for Social Development Research.

Wong, A. (2015, February 8). *The pros & cons of investing in commodities.* The Fifth Person. https://fifthperson.com/pros-cons-investing-commodities/

Woo, B., Rachemacher, I, & Meier, J. (2010). *Upside down: The $400 billion federal asset-building budget.* Corporation for Enterprise Development and the Annie E. Casey Foundation. https://community-wealth.org/content/upside-down-400-billion-federal-asset-building-budget

Wright, C.T. (2020). Black Buying Power By The Numbers: History In The Making. Retrieved December 25, 2021 from Black Buying Power By The Numbers: History In The Making | NewsOne

Yakoboski P., Lusardi A., & Hasler A. (2021). *Financial literacy, wellness and resilience among African Americans.* TIIA Institute. https://www.tiaainstitute.org/about/news/financial-literacy-wellness-and-resilience-among-african-americans

Made in the USA
Middletown, DE
10 January 2023

21858099R00118